John C. Thorns Jr

D0921525

CORPORATE DESIGN

by
Roger Yee and Karen Gustafson

INTERIOR
DESIGN
BOOKS

Published by Interior Design Books
A Division of Whitney Communications Corporation
850 Third Ave.
New York, NY 10022

Distributed by Van Nostrand Reinhold Company
135 West 50th Street
New York, NY 10020

Copyright © 1983 by Roger Yee and Karen Gustafson

ISBN 0-943370-01-9

All rights reserved. No part of this publication may be reproduced or transmitted in any form or by any means, electronic or mechanical, including photocopy, recording or any information storage and retrieval system, without permission in writing from the publisher.

First published in USA by Interior Design Books, a division of Whitney Communications Corporation, New York.

First published in Great Britain in 1983 by Thames and Hudson Ltd., London.

Designed by Balukas and Williams Design Group.

Marketing and Rights: Lusterman, Grybauskas Inc.

IDB Publications Director: Virginia Evans

IDB Publications Manager: Chris Duffy

Printed and bound in Japan by Dai Nippon Printing Company through DNP (America), Inc.

Library of Congress Cataloging in Publication Data

16   15   14   13   12   11   10   9   8   7   6   5   4   3   2   1

Yee, Roger.
  Corporate design.

  Bibliography: p.
  1. Office decoration—United States. 2. Office buildings—United States.
I. Gustafson, Karen. II. Title.
NK2195.04Y43   1983   725'.23   83-12592
ISBN 0-943370-01-9

CONTENTS

To our families

Carol and Philip
Martin and Amy

for their patience and support through the many
working evenings and weekends this book required.

Acknowledgments

Producing *Corporate Design* was very much like producing a corporate office. Beginning with a small group of assistants and advisers, the authors found themselves enlisting the aid of a growing number of people without whom the book could not have met its deadlines and our expectations. We would therefore like to acknowledge the contributions of some of the many individuals and organizations who helped us. Our thanks to Christine Duffy and Diana Riesman, who became our research department and indispensable aides; Judy Kalvin, Joanne Arevalo and Maria Skomsky, for typing, coordinating and other vital production matters; Virginia Evans, whose encouragement and supervision kept us on track; the interior designers, architects, photographers, manufacturers, museums, auction galleries, and building owners and managers, who generously gave us photographs and other valuable material to tell the story of *Corporate Design*; Roland Grybauskas and David Lusterman, for showing us how to turn our ideas into a book; Andrius Balukas and Stuart Williams, who turned countless photographs and manuscript pages into graphic design; Alberto Gavasci, David Lance and the art department of *Corporate Design* magazine and its sister publication, *Interior Design*, for preparing the photography that originally appeared in these magazines and some new art as well; Elizabeth Welch, who acted as our strict but enlightened copy editor; and the Beekman Delicatessen, for breakfasts, lunches and occasionally dinners too.

Roger Yee
Karen Gustafson
May 1983

I On Corporations and Real Estate

*"Land is about the only thing
that can't fly away."*
—ANTHONY TROLLOPE

It is a center of our intellectual and social life; it demands hours of concentrated effort; it provides close association with colleagues; it is a home away from home. The modern corporate office facility is all this in addition to being a complex work of architecture and interior design that is created by business wherever business opportunities justify it. Properly planned and executed, it can thrive virtually anywhere civilization does, which turns out to be a surprisingly small and fragile part of planet earth.

This may be difficult to evince on a weekday morning or afternoon in New York, London, Paris or Rome, when a beehive swarm of humanity engulfs the traffic lanes. From the height of a communication satellite orbiting some 22,300 miles above earth, civilization does look fairly precarious. Corporate offices and the rest of technological society cling tenaciously to coasts, inland bodies of water and key overland paths, leaving the expanses of continents and oceans as great voids. Man is gregarious, and his communities are dense and confined largely by choice, placing a premium on real estate even in the space age.

Our ability to penetrate deeper into the hinterlands is a measure of our ability to maintain lifelines to the coasts. The first wave of technological innovations carried us physically, as we exchanged travel by foot for travel by beast of burden, railroad, ship, automobile and aerospace craft. The next wave has brought new and uncertain possibilities to extend ourselves electronically, so that our thoughts race forward in the ether of telecommunications and computers while our bodies remain rooted to earth.

How far the technology of information processing will scatter our dense settlements will depend on how strongly we desire physical contact with one another. Already, instant and accurate data and voice transmission has helped make a world economy possible, so that buyer and seller can reach an agreement regardless of their respective geographic locations and time zones. In both the industrialized states and the developing ones, economic units as large as continents and as small as sole proprietorships are tying themselves to vast commercial and financial networks whose centers may be thousands of miles away.

Since technological know-how is proving almost impossible to confine within political borders, even advanced technological societies enjoy only a fleeting autumn in which to harvest their rewards before rivals invade their fields anew.[1] The critical factor for success in this world economy appears to be the adept use of timely information to formulate effective corporate strategy. Establishing and maintaining market share will take all the classic ingredients of a Horatio Alger story: business knowledge seasoned with experience, adequate capital, distinctive products or marketing, a smile from Dame Fortune—plus a constant stream of intelligence gathered from all directions by corporate personnel working in corporate offices.[2]

CRITERIA FOR THE WELL-MADE OFFICE

Why companies fail to handle information properly often begins with the traditional business bias for treating factories as capital goods

The location of a corporate office is primarily determined by whom the corporation must contact among its customers, suppliers and affiliates. In this view of Broad Street in New York, circa 1905, brokers unable to obtain seats on the New York Stock Exchange can be seen en masse conducting business on the curb across from the Exchange. From this curb, the American Stock Exchange was born. (Photograph from the Museum of the City of New York)

and offices as fixed overhead costs. When the mastering of manufacturing technique, achieving economy of scale and building distribution were the driving forces of industry, as they were in the 19th century, this bias was not unfounded. However, in a mature market-driven economy, the race no longer goes automatically to the swift, the colossal or the entrenched. Instead, the producer of the successful product, positioned for the right customer through marketing research and appropriate sales and distribution channels, takes the prize. Pulling off a marketing coup requires an office that can receive, store, retrieve, analyze and transmit information with the same care a factory gives raw materials and component parts.

The analogy of office and factory can be developed further. Though the principal capital goods in an office—people, business machines and information—differ profoundly from those of the factory—heavy machinery and materials—both have operating rules that affect output. The rules of the office are not so rigidly defined as those of the factory, of course. People are infinitely more flexible than machinery, and will find new ways to accomplish job tasks when the most efficient methods are precluded or unknown. Our inventiveness has rescued many an undeserving office and its company.

Setting forth planning criteria for a corporate facility is therefore less rigorous than it is for a factory. Quality is often traded off for expediency. However, to extract the most added value from the corporate office, a company must consider: location, personnel, size, ownership, space plans, office standards and aesthetics, and the symbolic power of real property.

LOCATION AS THE CORPORATE CAUSE CÉLÈBRE

Frost Belt versus Sun Belt, New York versus Houston, central city versus suburb: the location of an office facility in a specific region, metropolitan area and municipality will make some contacts with a company's other functioning units and outsiders easier and others more difficult. While cooperation between operating divisions varies from company to company, each unit large or small must orchestrate relationships with a sometimes populous chorus of outsiders. Besides suppliers and customers, its numbers may include commercial and investment bankers, attorneys, accountants, advertising agencies, competitors and government agencies. The question of location is complicated by other considerations that must be anticipated by a company, since they are commonly beyond its direct control: state and local laws, taxes and business attitudes, quality and availability of labor force, population trends, household statistics, unions, housing stock, office space inventory, job market, transportation, municipal services, cost of living, community life style and social conditions.

Qualify these issues with the frequent executive yearning for a prestigious address, a sylvan setting or the notorious five-minute drive to the home, country club or golf course, and location frequently flares into the cause célèbre of corporate facility planning. That it should never be allowed to become an emotional question is borne out by the many problems that emerge from a poor location decision: lack of contact with key customers, shortage of reasonably priced housing, few jobs for working spouses of employees, poor local infrastructure or absence of a nearby airport, to name a handful. Many management consultants believe more than half of all corporate location decisions are emotionally determined.

Despite the pitfalls of corporate location, American businesses have steadily dispersed their functioning units since the 1960s, moving their headquarters from central cities to the suburbs and from the Northeast and Midwest to the South and West, following the Interstate Highway System and airline routes to newer, less physically congested (or deteriorated), politically freer (or less heavily taxed) and more stable (or socially uniform) pastures. At the same time, more and more of these companies have been dividing what were once large centralized staffs into semi-autonomous parts: elite corporate headquarters, separate operating divisions and stand alone central administrative facilities.

Top business leaders often want easy personal access to one another, which is why most corporate headquarters remain in a handful of cities. High level negotiations are generally held face-to-face, for which cities excel. Gatherings such as the Harrison Grey Fiske dinner of 1900 in New York are still common today. (Photograph from the Museum of the City of New York)

Just as business creates jobs, a skilled work force makes business growth possible. Major corporate moves must consider the quality of personnel needed—and available. Service businesses are especially labor-intensive even in a computer age. Shown here is the office of George Borgfeldt & Co., Importers, New York, in 1910. (Photograph by Byron from the Museum of the City of New York)

Each of these functioning units, as management consultant Keith Wheelock has pointed out in *The New Dimensions of Office and Personnel Location* will locate where its own needs dictate rather than past historical circumstances.[3] Thanks to modern telecommunications and air travel, no unit will require proximity to another for merely exchanging routine information. A company desiring easy access to outside business leaders for its executives, for example, can house them in a small headquarters office in New York, Chicago or San Francisco. Heads of its operating divisions can be assigned to administrative offices close to their plants or markets. Central administrative services can be located to suit transportation, telecommunication or legal purposes in a distant location like Tulsa, Sioux Falls or Fairfax.

PERSONNEL LEAVE THE "BATTLESHIP"

The personnel stationed in a given corporate facility should consist mainly of those who require face-to-face contact and others who would strongly benefit from it. Judging from the continuing decentralization of businesses and their subsidiaries, executives have concluded that the various pieces of the corporate structure can afford to forsake face-to-face contact to gain greater freedom of action. As a consequence, new smaller facilities to shelter individual functioning units of personnel will probably outpace the traditional behemoth structures built earlier in the 20th century to house an army of headquarters employees. The transition from the "battleship" configuration, in which divisional heads are often tightly controlled by top executives at headquarters, to a "satellite" system, in which divisions enjoy considerable autonomy at their individual operating sites away from headquarters, parallels other fundamental changes in business.

Reasons for abandoning the battleship are many. Large multinational conglomerates frequently consist of businesses that are not closely related, hence gain little from proximity. Some industries demand close contact with major operations, markets or suppliers that

divisional heads must provide. Other companies have found information technology and travel to be satisfactory means for dispersing giant downtown staffs to gain flexibility and lower rents without losing administrative control.

Personnel size is not a handicap in itself, to be sure. Still, the history of the modern corporation, particularly the giant conglomerate dealing in numerous distinct lines of businesses, suggests that some size limit may exist at any one facility for effective management of separate businesses. Spinning off the components of a corporation into individual facilities is not a panacea for bad management; the record of many diversified companies in the 1970s and beyond, characterized by poor sales growth, overcapacity in mature markets, and inability to retain or increase market share in the face of strong competition, indicates that decisive action should have been taken at the operating divisional level—and was not.

SIZE AND FACILITY OBSOLESCENCE

A facility's size and complexity portray an educated guess of what a company needs at present and for the foreseeable future. So many factors can upset the best econometric models, however, that forecasting future facility requirements is at best an extremely problematic art. A facility could easily grow as sales increase, markets enlarge, other companies are acquired and folded in, or product lines broaden. On the other hand, poor financial results, restrictive government regulations, changing social conditions in the community or highly efficient office machines could actually shrink the facility.

Since most companies are inherently conservative in assessing future expenses, many routinely underestimate the size and complexity of the facilities they must occupy. The consequence of this hesitancy is inevitable. A large number of new offices are too small or otherwise obsolete by the time their occupants move in.

Management consultants frequently note that businesses could cushion themselves by overbuilding, subletting at a profit and gradually absorbing space as needed. This would

Good school systems make families more willing to accept a corporate location—and assure a continuing supply of skilled workers. Children of immigrants at the turn of the century benefited immensely from strong inner-city schools such as this Mott Street Industrial School of 1895. (Photograph by Jacob A. Riis from the Museum of the City of New York)

seem logical except that many non-real estate companies are loathe to think themselves involved in a real estate business when their main line of work could better use their resources. The outcome: many companies must rent additional space within a couple of years of their new facilities' completion, at considerably higher rates.

EQUITY VERSUS LEASING

Owning real estate poses a quandary for many non-real estate companies. Most lease space in speculative office buildings to free up precious capital for their principal businesses and to stay responsive to uncertain future business plans and space needs. Yet an equity position in the form of outright ownership, joint venture or limited partnership proffers certain advantages too: depreciation (tax write-off), cash flow (rent), appreciation (sale) and the right to custom tailor the facility to suit special needs. Though few companies manage their properties as astutely as their real estate executives would have them do, corporate fixed assets can be an unexpectedly useful source of cash, especially when all else fails.

SPACE PLANS, POLITICS AND COMMON SENSE

Space plans are drawn up by observing which organizational groups interact most and placing them as close together as possible on the available floors of the facility. Political considerations often play an important part in such details as who shall occupy the highest floor, enjoy the scenic view or be nearest to the exec-

utive suite. However, the group dynamics of most companies are self-evident even to outsiders. The consequences of overriding these natural affinities (such as the close ties between finance and accounting)—constant delays and inconveniences in daily operations—are usually enough to let common sense triumph over office politics.

It is very possible that this year's space plans will not suit next year's staff reorganization, however, and a measure of flexibility must be included in any office design. Certain types of private offices can be designed for two, three or more occupants; areas that may need private offices in the future can be let open for general staff meanwhile; demountable walls can be used in place of permanent ones. Companies can also build or lease space that can be partly sublet and then absorbed or can hold options in their office buildings to lease more space at a specified later date.

Even today's best space plans will pinch like a child's old shoe if neglected for any considerable period of time. Companies typically assign new people to spaces wherever vacancies occur. This gradually erodes the integrity of working relationships within their organizations, if not corrected by careful revisions to existing space plans on a periodic basis.

OFFICE STANDARDS: IS IMAGE TRIVIAL?

Office standards and aesthetics are the rules by which space, equipment and amenities are allotted according to job title, demonstrable need and corporate protocol. Like location, office standards can easily become an emo-

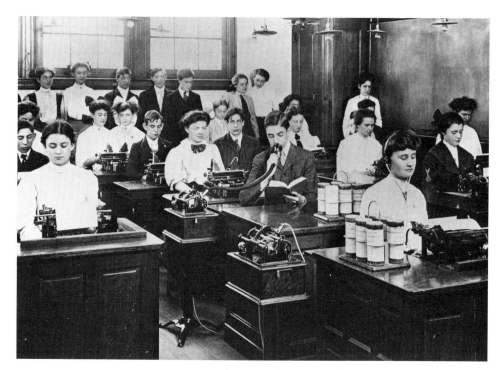

The widespread use of business machines has had profound and continuing consequences for the planning of corporate facilities, as each new wave of information technology intensifies the concentration of information processing power. In this 1906 New York high school, students are studying Dictaphone, typing and stenography. (Photograph by Byron from the Museum of the City of New York)

Transportation affects two key business factors: how easy it is to reach a given destination and how long it will take to get there. The private automobile has given America considerable mobility in the 20th century, yet mass transit still remains the most efficient way to concentrate large numbers of people. This photograph shows a women-only subway car in New York in 1909. (Photograph from Culver Pictures)

tional issue in corporate facility planning. Who is entitled to how much space? Who gets a private window office? What pieces of furniture will each employee receive? How will the aesthetic appearance of the facility be determined?

The answers to these questions should be based largely on demonstrable need. Unfortunately, since every company is politically stratified into groups having more or less power and status, floor space and furnishings cannot always be awarded meritoriously. Corporate attorneys, for example, are extremely sensitive to the size and appointments of their offices; they seldom accept anything less than private window space.

What business people sometimes overlook is that the same factors that equip companies for work also define the image the company projects to its staff and its outside publics. The determination of the architecture, engineering, interior design, building materials, office machines and office furnishings are no less trivial than the principles they embody. Among these principles are management style, team spirit, corporate ethics, professional quality, civic responsibility and self-esteem.

Every form of human labor, no matter how cerebral, requires some form of tool to complete. Even Mozart, fabled for composing extended musical compositions completely in his mind, would eventually reach for paper and ink to transcribe them. Denying office workers the proper "tools of the trade" hampers their ability to process information accurately, efficiently and creatively.

Beyond pure function, office standards and aesthetics are a litmus test of an employer's attitudes. When the office functions properly, when it provides the appropriate equipment for getting the job done and a pleasant setting for the rituals of office life that occupy half our waking hours, employees are positively reinforced in their efforts to represent the company's best interests. When things go consistently wrong, it is hard to escape the impression that the causes of the problems are either unknown to the company or beyond its power. Either way, the image created is of a company going out of control.

REAL PROPERTY AS WEALTH AND POWER

Both primitive man and the higher primates have come to blows over three basic commodities, according to Dr. David Hamburg, medical research scientist and president of the Carnegie Corporation (*The World Transformed: Critical Issues in Contemporary Human Adaptation*), namely land, food and females.[4] One could say modern man has not improved his conduct significantly, for he still esteems land as a primary source of wealth and power worth fighting for. Land continues to function as the sustaining medium for all our material culture.

In fact, our relationship to the land has become exceedingly convoluted. Hunter-gatherer peoples roam across vast territories, pausing only to extract each day's nutrition before moving on. Sedentary peoples employing more sophisticated agricultural techniques survey strict boundaries to protect their long and costly nurturing of the land. Technological society is so acutely aware of the shortage of desirable locations for farming and industry that it plants a thicket of zoning laws, building codes, historic landmark designations and environmental regulations on real property to safeguard its usefulness. Real property still

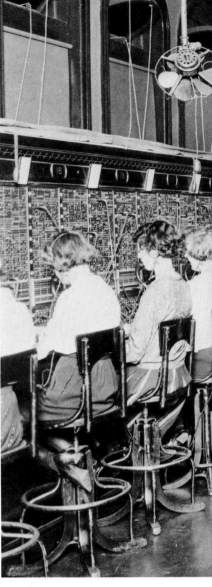

Superior telephone service, which can now be taken for granted across the United States, was mostly restricted to central cities early in the 20th century—putting one more limit on corporate location and mobility. The central telephone exchange of Kansas City (MO) can be seen in this 1904 view. (Photograph reproduced with permission of AT&T)

exercises a unique power over our affairs.

The sheer physical presence of a corporate office, for example, proclaims it a force to be reckoned with. Much as a medieval sovereign, such as England's King John (1199–1216), visited some 100 royal residences in his realm each year to control his vassals, business executives build offices in key locations where they intend to conduct significant transactions. A corporate office asserts its company's citizenship in a given business community. It is a stake no frequency of out-of-town visits could duplicate.

Having a custom-made "home" in a given location also bestows the privileges of the "home owner" to a company: privacy, comfort, refuge and the right to conduct and control face-to-face relationships with outsiders by manipulating the office environment to

support a business plan or strategy. Renting a hotel suite provides some but not all of these privileges.

And real property as an asset wears an unmistakable aura of respectability, since property has always been a fundamental means of storing wealth for most of the world's peoples. A corporation's name on an office door or, better yet, a building facade is a financial statement of its net worth. Visitors may well know the veracity of this statement; nevertheless, first impressions tend to be lasting ones.

FORM AND/OR FUNCTION

What could be more logical than a chair: carrying live weight off the ground, resisting side-sway and racking stress, enduring lifting, dropping and tilting. Yet few objects point up so consistently mankind's reluctant submission to pure reason. Were a chair truly nothing more than a paean to human anatomy and physiology, as architects and designers of the Modern movement insisted (the Belgium architect Henry van de Velde said in 1903, "It will take us a long time to recognize the exact form of a table, a chair, a house."), then there should not have been the proliferation of highly idiosyncratic chair designs that are civilization's unending bequest to us.[5] Our anatomy has not changed significantly in millions of years; there is little new to add to the anthropometric data compiled by Nicholas Andry de Boisregard in his *L'Orthopedie* of 1741.[6]

In truth, we vary the form of our artifacts even when their functions are similar because *what* we do in society attains significance only when others know *who* we are. Pouring water from a pitcher has very different meanings when the person pouring it is identified as a nurse, a waiter or a priest. Man's artifacts—the material objects he fashions to facilitate his rituals—give him the public identity he needs to perform his office. These artifacts embrace virtually the entire manmade environment.

Great leaders have instinctively recognized and exploited the eloquence of visual forms in projecting their identities, particularly the magnitude and legitimacy of their status and power. The desire to create and control a specific public image can result in such extremes as a thatched cottage at Osaka Castle, in which the legendary 16th century Japanese warlord Toyotomi Hideyoshi personally served tea to his favorite generals, or a glittering 320-foot long *Grand Galerie* (the "Hall of Mirrors") built by Louis XIV in that extravagance of 17th-century French architecture, Versailles.

Thus, form does not follow function in any absolute Platonic sense, and human cultures, guided by learning rather than instinct, respond to their particular circumstances by surrounding truly universal social functions such as eating, sleeping or washing with artifacts and rituals that are distinctly their own. Our responses to these universal functions make us uniquely American, Japanese or other nationalities, as anthropologist Margaret Mead repeatedly demonstrated in her national character studies of the Allies and the Axis Powers in World War II.[7] There is no "perfect" solution to any functional problem. To a Roman field commander, a chair was a folding stool with wood stretchers and a cloth seat; to a Moorish prince, it was a cushion on a carpeted floor; to an American executive, it is a swivel arm chair in leather, steel, aluminum and plastic.

Civilization's explorations in visual forms remind us that aesthetics play a crucial role in defining our organizations. Far from being arbitrary, the forms we create fuse complex social values into highly charged symbols meant to inspire and reinforce group identities. For a contemporary corporation, the location, architecture and interior design of its corporate office facilities are part of its institutional clothing, along with its people, factories

Although cost of living, state and local taxes and quality of education are important factors in the ability of business to attract good personnel to a particular location, growth industries like computers have found that life style is also highly significant, since highly educated workers seek cultural and recreational opportunities where they live. Here is a glimpse of a fox hunt in progress with the Meadowbrook Hounds, Hempstead, Long Island, in 1899. (Photograph by Byron from the Museum of the City of New York)

Adequate and affordable housing can control the growth of commerce. Companies that overlook this may find themselves in the housing business, buying and selling for their employees. New York's famed "Millionaires' Row" is visible in this look up Fifth Avenue taken in 1898. (Photograph by Byron from the Museum of the City of New York)

and products. How they look and fit depend on the leadership's image of what the organization is—or should become.

THE CORPORATE IDENTITY CRISIS

When a salesman gestures towards the sorriest looking model on the showroom floor and pipes up, "It's functional," we all know his hidden meaning. Calling something "functional" is like describing someone as "plain." The term masks a skeptical attitude regarding aesthetics behind a facade of straightforward utility. To be "functional" insinuates that the object in question is dull and uninteresting because anything better looking would be wasteful and encumbering. The trouble with this argument is that nearly everything is "functional."

If the modern corporation intends to foster a favorable opinion of itself in society, it needs more than a "functional" image. If anything, it needs a strong visual image. Otherwise, it stands in constant danger of having no image at all.

By transcending its entrepreneurial personalities, rough-and-tumble management style and vertically integrated structures in the first decade of the 20th century, the modern corporation has evolved into an increasingly disparate, finance-oriented collection of semi-autonomous operating divisions that can easily be attached or spun off. The paramount role of the corporate headquarters continues to isolate the corporation's leadership from its tangible sources of power and wealth, the capital assets and personnel of its divisions, and these sources from each other. Thus, the identity of a corporation, its headquarters staff, divisions, products and services, can be vague or even unknown to the public. A proliferation of abstract corporate names and logotypes and a growing tendency for products and services to become similar in nature regardless of their origin has only compounded the problem. Establishing a convincing identity for the contemporary corporate office facility is a challenge that should be taken for the sake of the corporation's own personnel if no one else's.

II   Corporate Architecture

"The Cathedral of Commerce!"
—*SAMUEL PARKES CADMAN*

In America's love affair with tall buildings, few skyscrapers will be welcomed as the Woolworth Building was. On the mild and moonless evening of April 24, 1913, thousands of spectators gathered at New York's City Hall Park as a procession of carriages and limousines entered the financial district, destined for Broadway and Park Place. There, some 900 men, prominent in business, government, the arts and sciences, were ushered into an improvised banquet hall on the building's twenty-seventh floor. At 7:30 the lights of the building were lowered. President Woodrow Wilson pressed a button in the White House in Washington, 80,000 lights surged on, and America's latest architectural achievement—a Gothic skyscraper and the world's tallest building—stood out like a burning sword against the evening sky. As the crowd roared, Dr. Samuel Parkes Cadman, a prominent clergyman with a fondness for rhetoric, cried out "The Cathedral of Commerce!"[1]

The skyscraper is perhaps America's only original contribution to the world's architecture. Like jet aircraft and computers, it is a technological *tour de force* for which the United States has few peers. At its best, it is economic pragmatism joined to artistic imagination in a union that almost if not quite transcends its purpose, the drive for profit. Only a little over a century ago, business sired it, architecture bore it, and engineering delivered it to a young and sprawling nation that sought space in the sky when the limitations of technology would not permit it to expand outward. When technology completed the conquest of the land, the skyscraper obediently tilted on its side and spread out instead of up.

For the skyscraper—or less poetically, the office building—has been dedicated to the needs of business from the moment business summoned it into existence.

There was no office building to speak of at the dawn of the Industrial Revolution, in the second half of the 18th century. Office space as it existed was contained within royal households and merchants' and artisans' residences. Production was limited to men and their primitive machines, and distribution was restricted by barriers to transportation, communication and free trade. Business administration was a relatively uncomplicated activity.

When inventors and entrepreneurs such as Wedgwood, Boulton and Watt built factories, it was still possible to find room for the office behind the machinery and the toiling laborers, a pattern that persisted well into the 19th century. The need to invent and practice more proficient techniques of mass production kept management preoccupied with the factory at first. However, with the canals, railroads, telegraph and national magazines came national markets, vertical integration, and the need to coordinate production with finance, distribution, sales and advertising. The home office needed a home of its own near other companies' home offices.

An early solution was the so-called business block, a rectilinear masonry and wood construction that seldom rose higher than six stories. Its size was established by the modest requirements of its occupants, who generally occupied floors of a few thousand square feet. The owner's name in raised lettering on the main facade pediment added to the building's character, as did the long walk up its stairs.

The Woolworth Building of 1913 in New York was designed by Cass Gilbert to give Frank W. Woolworth, chief executive of the famous five-and-ten retail chain, the tallest building in the world as his headquarters. Woolworth paid $13 million out of his own pocket for the privilege of being tallest. Gilbert created a tower for him in the Gothic style that rises magisterially from its base, a "Cathedral of Commerce" that has been carefully restored by The Ehrenkrantz Group. (Photograph by Morris Rosenfeld, reproduced with permission of AT&T)

The Metropolitan Life Insurance building of 1906 in New York was designed by Napoleon Le Brun and Sons, and became an instant symbol for the insurance giant. From its tower was broadcast the famed "Light that Never Fails." (Photograph courtesy of Metropolitan Life Insurance Co.)

From the middle of the 19th century to its close, the accelerating pace of economic development called for a new kind of structure with greater technical capabilities. Captains of industry such as Morgan, Carnegie and Rockefeller created organizations of unprecedented size and complexity that functioned most efficiently in densely occupied central business districts of cities such as New York and Chicago. Here, where railroads and sea lanes converged, telephone systems ran smoothly, and retail and cultural amenities were first rate, business leaders could hold face-to-face meetings supported by a phalanx of bankers, attorneys, accountants, and advertising agencies, and an army of office workers drawn from a populous metropolitan region.

Growing demand for this superior business environment forced land values in these districts to soar and thereby sweetened the incentive to find ways to intensify land use. The answer was to stack people up to the sky. To build a building capable of doing this took two key technological inventions: a safe elevator and high-quality steel in large quantities. Both were available by the turn of the century.

GROWING TALLER THROUGH TECHNOLOGY

The elevator, whose safety had been demonstrated by inventor Elisha Otis in 1854, removed the curse of height and transformed the penalty of walking up to the highest story into a premium of sunlight and views. Iron and steel, in continuous use since 1500 B.C. and 1000 B.C. respectively but only available in bulk in the 1850s, severed the ancient architectural unity of structure and cladding by

LEFT *The Empire State Building of 1931 in New York by Shreve, Lamb and Harman, an offspring of the Depression, sat empty until World War II, but made a lasting impression as the world's tallest building—and a perch for King Kong. Dirigibles never reached its tower as intended; however, a U.S. Army B-25 bomber did on July 28, 1945—destroying itself but not the building. (Photograph courtesy of Empire State Building)* RIGHT *Rockefeller Center of 1931-39 in New York by Reinhard and Hofmeister;*

Corbett, Harrison and MacMurray; Hood and Fouilhoux, was financed by John D. Rockefeller Jr. in the depths of the Depression as a sign of faith in the nation's economy and an intended home for the Metropolitan Opera. When it was completed, it constituted one of the most splendid collections of skyscrapers in the world. Inside is a complex city within a city of offices, shops, entertainment and passageways running beneath Manhattan's streets. (Photograph courtesy of Rockefeller Center Inc.)

planting a self-supporting framework within walls relieved of the responsibility of carrying themselves—much less the entire building. Suddenly, the limitations of stone piled upon stone, reached when Daniel Burnham and John Wellborn Root designed Chicago's Monadnock Building in brick, 1889-91, with 16 stories and walls four feet thick at the base, could be breached.

A desire to give original aesthetic expression to steel rather than dry academic recitals of Classic orders inspired the Chicago school of architecture to create new forms for stretch-ing the old building block ever higher. One of the most successful attempts was Louis Sullivan's 12-story Guaranty Building of 1894-95 in Buffalo, which defined its ascending mass as a logical sequence of events starting with a sturdy entrance floor base, proceeding to a vertically oriented shaft of office floors, and capped by a service floor and cornice, a procession not unlike the Greek or Roman column in spirit.

In the 20th century, economic incentive and engineering theory were joined to another kind of purpose in the minds of corporate

LEFT *The Seagram Building of 1958 in New York by Mies van der Rohe and Philip Johnson was the quintessential International Style modern skyscraper in slab form. By being designed and built to the most refined proportions and workmanship, it equated the House of Seagram with uncompromising quality. (Photograph by Alexandre Georges)* CENTER *The John Hancock Center of 1969 in Chicago by Skidmore, Owings & Merrill, Chicago, is a technological image of structural engineering in action, with its di-* agonal bracing that is visible on the facade. (Photograph courtesy of John Hancock Mutual Life Insurance Company)* RIGHT *Pennzoil Place of 1974 in Houston by Philip Johnson and John Burgee was not the tallest building in the nation's energy center even when it was planned. Yet the idiosyncratic and handsome twin trapezoidal towers and their glass courtyard stood out at once. (Photograph by © Richard Payne AIA)*

leaders and their architects in New York, who pursued still higher altitudes than Chicago's. The high rise tower lifting itself from a low rise base made its appearance here because sheer height for its own sake fired the imaginations of the city's entrepreneurs. Corporations vied like athletes for the honor of building the world's tallest skyscraper: Singer Building of 1908 (621 feet) by Ernest Flagg, Metropolitan Life Insurance Building of 1909 (700 feet) by Napoleon Le Brun and Sons, Woolworth Building of 1913 (792 feet) by Cass Gilbert, Chrysler Building of 1930 (1046 feet) by Wil-

liam Van Alen and Empire State Building of 1931 (1250 feet) by Shreve, Lamb and Harman. New York became, in the words of art historian Vincent Scully in *American Architecture and Urbanism,* "a city of genial giants."[2]

Two more major office building configurations would take their places beside the tower before the Depression cut short these forays in corporate image making: the stepped back "ziggurat" and its descendant, a progressively more flattened "slab." The mountain-like massing of the ziggurat, perhaps most nobly represented by a design submitted to the Chicago Tribune Building competition of 1922 by Eliel Saarinen, allowed the tower to emerge gracefully from a solid rectilinear base by shedding its mass in stages. The slab gave business a bold new shape that maximized the amount of window exposure its occupants could enjoy. The last significant collaborative project between art and architecture in the glorification of commerce, industry and technology was designed in slab form: Rockefeller Center of 1931–39 in New York by Reinhard and Hofmeister; Corbett, Harrison and Mac-Murray; Hood and Fouilhoux, probably the finest complex of skyscrapers ever constructed.

THE CITY COMES TO THE COUNTRY

The resumption of office building in the 1940s brought a very different kind of urban design to the landscape, only this time to the suburbs as well as the cities. Continuing decentralization of the nation's transporation, energy and communication networks from the cities, which began in the 1920s, dulled the appeal of a central business district address. So did the spread of high quality business services, which followed their customers out of town. The suburbs defined the American Dream on their own terms: a life of work and play revolving around the detached single-family home on its own plot of land, isolated by open space from the conflicting influences of factories, offices and shopping. By the 1960s, unable to offer an alternative vision and helpless to stem the flight of all but the poorest of their citizens, the cities watched in dismay and anger as many companies relocated their offices, jobs and taxable income beyond city limits.[3]

Inevitably, suburban office workers and their employers preferred to work closer to home, and office buildings were needed to satisfy them. What would a suburban "campus"-style office building look like? Numerous prototypes existed. The factory building of the 1930s and 1940s had evolved under such gifted architects as Albert Kahn into an incredibly vast and exciting pavilion of raw space pierced by windows and skylights. The Johnson Wax headquarters of 1936–39 in Racine (WI) by Frank Lloyd Wright set its occupants down in a forest of Minoan columns bathed in light and space. The campus for the Illinois Institute of Technology of 1940–56 in Chicago by Mies van der Rohe let its students roam amidst tautly stretched blocks of space machined in steel, glass and brick that seemed more elysian than inner city in spirit as they glided over grassy lawns. And so the pattern was set for long, low sprawling structures such as the elegant headquarters of John Deere & Co. of 1961–64 in Moline (IL) by Eero Saarinen.

The city office building has followed a curious life of its own. Architects refining the slab form after Rockefeller Center continue to produce distinguished works like the Seagram Building of 1956–58 in New York by Mies van der Rohe and Philip Johnson, while those furthering the tower theme have created such distinctive designs as the John Hancock Building of 1969 in Chicago by Skidmore, Owings and Merrill. Yet variations on these basic types began to appear in the 1970s when business people and their architects deliberately sought more idiosyncratic shapes for no apparent reason other than novelty, such as the twin trapezoid towers of Pennzoil Place of 1971–73 in Houston by Philip Johnson and John Burgee. As was true at the beginning of the 20th century, corporate architecture is not shaped by logic alone.

A BUILDING FOR EVERY BUSINESS

Like a starry-eyed lover, the corporation that takes space in an office building without testing its plans and elevations for compatibility has a surprise in store once the honeymoon is over. If architecture is an artistic synthesis of economic, political, social and technical circumstances, then some office buildings will surely pose more sympathetic conditions to a corporation's cause than others. It pays to ask first.

• **Planning module** is the basic length that generates a building's dimensions. For most office buildings, the module is five feet, which happens to be the length of a standard office desk.

• **Bay size** is the fundamental rectangular

United States Trust Company of 1982 in New York by Haines, Lundberg, Waehler was one of a growing number of renovations of existing structures that took advantage of the materials and craftsmanship of the past in solving the needs of the present by restoring a pair of neo-Georgian townhouses designed in 1896 for James J. Goodwin by McKim, Mead & White. (Photograph by George Cserna)

floor area framed by four columns. This represents the largest unit of space that is free of columns, which must be considered in laying out offices, aisles and open spaces.

- **Floor size** is the total square footage on a floor. The amount varies with the qualifications; it could include or exclude such spaces as common areas, utility closets, elevators or fire stairs. Overall floor dimensions are also worth noting for the distance and thus the time required to walk from one end of the floor to the other.

- **Floor shape** cannot always be assumed to be purely quadrangular. Building owners have become more adventurous in allowing floors with curves, zigzags and acutely angled corners. Some shapes can be highly efficient, having little wasted space, despite complex geometries. But rectangular floors tend to be consistently usable.

- **Window wall to core depth** is the distance from the perimeter of a building to its core, the rigid bundle of vertically distributed utilities in a building, such as elevators, fire stairs, plumbing and risers for air, power and communications. This distance determines how many layers of work stations can be planned along a given side of a building.

- **Core size** is the square footage on a floor lost to utilities. The amount is usually greatest on the lower floors of a tall building owing to the many elevators that pass through.

- **Core location** shows how core services will be distributed horizontally on a floor. A core at the center will generally feed all areas with equidistant runs, whereas a core at one extreme will probably not.

- **Number of floors** is relevant when compared with floor size since its establishes how a company's functioning groups will be deployed on various levels, the so-called "stacking" plan.

- **Elevators** join strings of consecutive floors together. In high rise buildings, they segregate floors into separate zones for greater efficiency of service; this can inconvenience a company with space served by different elevators.

- **Building configuration** continues to be a variation on the themes of building block, tower, slab and campus. As shown by their evolution, each has its legitimacy for certain companies and locations. The building block, slab and older tower are well suited to smaller companies. The contemporary tower, whose floor size often dwarfs the tower of 1900–1940, and campus tend to serve larger companies better. Where each form is located is generally a function of economics and politics, with conspicuous exceptions to the rule made largely for marketing effect.

ARCHITECTURAL STYLE OR PACKAGING?

Long before any Modern designer ventured out of the nursery, matters had gone terribly wrong for the design profession. When William Morris, English designer and founder of the Arts and Crafts movement, attended an international exhibition of consumer products at London's Crystal Palace in 1851, he found everything "wonderfully ugly." Manufacturers had borrowed period styles with little conviction or sympathy and combined them in hopes of giving their machines something new and valuable to reproduce. The Modern school blossomed from attempts by Morris and others to conceive a new aesthetic language appropriate to the machine age.

Although the results of this creative outburst failed to provide any single all encompassing solution for our time—changing technological needs being antithetical to the maturation of great artistic movements of the past—Western society was at last free to pursue as many aesthetic destinies as it wanted or needed. If high technology packaging or Queen Anne style meant nothing to the engineering beneath the veneer, then anything

Oak Industries of 1981 in Rancho Bernardo (CA) by Dale Naegle Architecture and Planning and Brenda Mason Design Associates houses the electronics and communications company in a faithful reproduction of architecture from California's Mexican colonial period (1521-1820). The company relocated from the Midwest. (Photograph by Charles Schneider)

John Deere & Co. of 1964 in Moline (IL) by Eero Saarinen and Associates was a major achievement in the defining of the suburban office building in that its sensitive placement on its site and the graceful articulation of its parts set a high standard and demonstrated that the skyscraper was not the only way to make a convincing corporate statement. (Photograph courtesy of Kevin Roche John Dinkeloo and Associates

Best Products of 1980 in Richmond (VA) by Hardy, Holzman, Pfeiffer is an eclectic and intriguing image that combines details of Greco-Roman architecture, Art Deco glass block in a diamond mosaic pattern, and two massive eagles that once surmounted the Airlines Terminal Building of 1939 in New York, which aggressively flank the main entrance. (Photograph by Norman McGrath)

would do. And indeed, the rigid aesthetic standards of taste so prevalent in Western culture up to the first half of the 20th century have been almost totally dismantled. A price has been exacted for this dispensation, however; much of the new man-made environment is completely lacking in charm or grace. The absence of clear definitions of style makes the choices even harder to distinguish.

Modern design in all its variations is sought by many corporations as their institutional image because the Modern style is thoroughly accepted by the giants of the business community. Imposing Modern design on a wide range of physical environments around the planet is not unlike dropping man on the moon, since environmental controls may be heavily used to allow a Modern building to maintain a liveable interior. However, many corporations anxious for the "Big Business" look willingly pay the cost.

Regional design acknowledges indigenous conditions, taking into account the local environment, native materials and traditional building techniques in producing a contemporary image. The results are not necessarily much different from Modern design, but the aesthetic decisions are made with less doctrinaire insistence and greater environmental sensitivity and individual character.

Period or historic styles may be adopted to suggest that the corporation is older and more established than it is. One could believe that business leaders who build facilities in English Georgian or Spanish Colonial styles truly identify with the philosophies of these eras. More likely, they simply yearn for a sense of tradition that takes longer than they can afford. Given the velocity of change in technological society, the question of period style is a most quintessential dilemma for today.

Architectural style is inevitably an arbitrary cultural choice. Everything that occurs under the surface of style, by contrast, is much more deliberate. And yet, the size or shape of a floor, the number of stories and the proportions of a facade are neither wholly fact or fantasy. An office building is paradoxically more and less than its corporation and its architect claim it to be.

Integon headquarters of 1982 in Winston-Salem (NC) by Welton Beckett, Chicago, houses the insurance subsidiary of Ashland Oil in a structure designed to conserve energy and to respect the venerable First Baptist Church across the street. (Photograph by Gordon Schenck)

Meredith Corp. headquarters of 1981 in Des Moines (IO) is a renovation by Charles Herbert and Associates that unifies years of additions to an original building of 1911. The tower and base contrast sharply with the new facade of glass and aluminum. The project expresses Meredith's conservative family values and progressive marketing. (Photograph by Architectural Fotographics/Paul S. Kivett)

American Telephone & Telegraph's Long Lines Eastern Region headquarters of 1981 in Oakton (VA) by Kohn, Pedersen, Fox is an organization of expandable office space units or "pods" tied to a main circulation corridor or "galleria" whose eastern entrance is shown here. The scheme establishes a strong internal focus for the low, sprawling structure in its rural setting. (Photograph by © Ezra Stoller/Esto)

Hollister headquarters of 1982 in Libertyville (IL) by Holabird & Root ties offices, laboratories and computers together with a nave-like atrium. The high technology image seems apt for a health care company. (Photograph by Sarah Lavicka)

McDonnell Douglas Automation Company (MCAUTO) of 1981 in St. Louis by Hellmuth, Obata & Kassabaum was designed to meet founder James S. McDonnell's challenge to house the computer services headquarters in a building that "won't look old 100 years from now." Actually seven structures performing four distinct functions, MCAUTO is a tour de force *in high technology forms and bright electric colors. (Photograph by Nathan Benn)*

OPPOSITE
Georgia Power Co. headquarters of 1981 in Atlanta by Heery & Heery demonstrates the company commitment to energy conservation. An active solar system of 1,482 parabolic trough collectors covers the low-rise rooftop adjoining the office tower that protrudes 23 feet farther on the top than the bottom—for shade from the summer sun. (Photograph by Timothy Hursley © The Arkansas Office)

RIGHT
Texas Commerce Tower of 1982 in Houston by I.M. Pei & Partners (design) and 3D/International (production and interiors) was built to house the holding company of one of the nation's fastest growing and most profitable regional banks. The distinctive shape of the 75-story structure came from slicing one corner from its square floor plan to "face" the city's bustling southwest quadrant. (Photograph by © 1982 Nathaniel Lieberman)

OVERLEAF *Warner Bros. headquarters of 1981 in Burbank (CA) by the Luckman Partnership and Swimmer, Cole, Martinez, Curtis, situated across the street from Jack Warner's 1926 administration building, allows production units to expand and contract as movies progress to completion. Executive offices have balconies tucked in the curving facade. (Photograph by Wes Thompson)*

III Corporate Interiors

*"We shape our buildings
and they shape us."*
SIR WINSTON CHURCHILL

Ideally, buildings should be built from the inside out, by first evaluating the needs of the users and then designing the building to meet those needs. It seems obvious, yet all too often corporate egos or an architect's "vision" get in the way of creating a workable facility and the building that is the talk of the town is also the subject of its inhabitants' complaints. Or the bottom line dictates the building and the result is a structure that lacks space, amenities *and* inspiration. The irony is that people are the real costs in an organization. No matter what the cost of the building, its finishing and furniture, it is still a fraction of the cost of developing and keeping talented employees.

Because people experience themselves in terms of their environment, the spatial setting for work influences (for better or for worse) the work experience. Edward Hall, the anthropologist, stresses that man's experience of space is not visual alone, but multisensory and related to action.[1] The best architects and designers know this. In their buildings people interact with space—moving from grand-scale public areas to personal-scale work areas, touching a rough stone wall, stepping on smooth carpeting, seeing a brightly colored kimono hung as art, smelling freshly watered plants, or hearing water falling onto pebbles. The presence of sensory stimuli gives a work setting grace and lets employees know that someone cares how they feel as well as how they produce. (The more desirable employees will especially appreciate these "extras.") Yet we are interested in how well employees produce—particularly in how corporate facilities help or hinder productivity.

Worker effectiveness studies to date have concentrated on industrial rather than office environments. Certainly it is easier to measure the number of widgits coming off a production line than it is to quantify the effectiveness of office work. CRT operators can be monitored by their own machines—the CRT keeping count of the number of errors made and the work time for each project.

But creative and professional jobs are not so easy to measure. Whistling a happy tune might be the depressurizer that allows a writer or artist's juices to flow, while an executive might find staring out the window helps him come to a decision. Neither activity appears to be work, but both are valid work processes.

Since product quality and quantity in the office cannot effectively be measured, recent research has looked at attendance, efficiency, human development and human costs, with worker satisfaction with the work situation recognized as an important performance consideration. Among its many aspects is "the effectiveness of the functional organization network—the way in which people relate to one another and to services and other facilities."[2] Research has also shown that satisfaction with the environment is closely associated with self-related job performance.[3]

The reason satisfaction with one's work environment is important is that one's job function (the job title and job tasks) is closely linked with the form of one's job. On a *practical* level, the form is that part of the facility that permits the worker to perform the job. If one is an executive, one might have a desk, a personal chair, a couple of visitor's chairs, storage space and certainly a telephone. These

The atrium of Diamond Shamrock's Industrial Chemicals Group in Dallas provides every employee in the all open plan facility with a view of greenery, natural light, and the soothing sound of falling water. Designed by Harwood K. Smith & Partners. (Photograph by Hursley/Lark/Hursley)

The offices of Mid-Atlantic Toyota in Glen Burnie (MD) are kept as open as possible to encourage interaction among its people. Walls typically encircle space without enclosing it. Seated in one of the more private offices is the vice president of the company. Designed by Frank O. Gehry and Associates. (Photograph by Ron Solomon)

would be the basics. But then there is the level of *symbolic* form where the quality of these basics plus extras express the importance of the worker's job title.

For example, if the executive is a senior vice president in charge of finance, he might report directly to the president and work closely with the vice presidents and senior management. He might also receive bank officers and other outsiders in his office. Because his internal and external images are seen as the company's image, it is important for the company that his office be impressive.

And it is important for the executive himself since his office is symbolic of the recognition he has earned. Just as scouts receive merit badges as a symbolic reward for their actions, so executives in America's corporations receive larger offices, more windows, bigger and better furnishings, and perhaps even a private bathroom.

Yet for most workers symbolic form is hardly the issue—they are still struggling to get the basics. For them the work environment is frustrating. Sometimes they are not sure why—they just know it is not right—it does not support their work effort.

In the remainder of this section, we will look at different aspects of the work environment to understand how it reflects management philosophy, bestows status, increases one's power, and helps and/or hinders the work effort. We will discuss location, dimensions of space and workers, entrance and enclosure, privacy, controlling the environment, territorial distance, color and lighting.

LOCATION

The most desirable work locations in the company are those situated closest to the command center of the organization. If the senior vice president has the president's ear, his office will most likely be in the executive row close to the president's own; or better yet, he will have a corner office. Often, the powers in an organization are found in each corner office, with the boardroom occupying the central spot where their lines of power cross. Therefore, the closer to the corner, the greater one's

At the Xerox Corporation headquarters in Stamford (CT) the executive reception area is rich in art: a Chinese Mandarin robe embroidered in silk; an onyx sculpture by Norma Flannagan; and a fiber work by Lewis Knauss. Interior design by ISD Incorporated. (Photograph by Jaime Ardiles-Arce)

importance. Michael Korda (*Power! How to get it, how to use it*) even suggests it may be wiser to stay inside the power area, foregoing a windowed office in the middle of the row, until one can have a corner office of one's own.[4]

Many companies today are opting for open office planning and are democratically placing the open plan work stations adjacent to the windows. If the vice presidents and upper management are on the same floor, their offices will typically be *enclosed* by ceiling-height walls at the interior of the floor with a window or window wall facing the light-filled general office area. (In this case being positioned away from the masses indicates status.) It is interesting to note, however, that the president and chairman usually retain exterior windowed offices. Democracy only goes so far!

Diamond Shamrock's Industrial Chemicals Group in Dallas has one of the few facilities where *all* executives are in open plan offices. And Northwest Energy Corporation in Salt Lake City has even convinced its legal department to accept open plan. Both companies have given its employees visual bonuses as compensation: Diamond Shamrock situated a rain forest of an atrium in the very center of its building, while Northwest Energy built walls of glass to showcase its mountain views. Where the executives sit usually reflects the goals of management. While isolation in enclosed offices may increase status, some managers might profit from closer interaction with the people they supervise and/or their peers.

Location status is vertical as well as horizontal. Generally, the higher the floor, the higher one's status. One company's space dilemma was supposedly solved by a computer that could analyze stacking plans (where departments are located floor by floor). Originally the executives had the top (eighth) floor,

The colors at the San Paolo Bank in New York are comforting to work by because they are neither too contrasting nor reflective. The design itself by architects Voorsanger & Mills is termed Post-Modern because of its use of color and newly constructed architectural forms. (Photograph by © Peter Aaron/Esto)

but as departments shifted a couple floors were left with unused space. The computer's solution completely reshuffled the company, freeing the top floor to be leased and placing the executives on the second floor. The computer considered everything except the symbolic perk of being king of the mountain.

DIMENSIONS

Hierarchy within an organization is most often indicated by the size of one's work area. American corporations usually provide employees with the minimum amount of space needed for the job. Anything more is status recognition. While "feeling cramped" is not measurable data, Edward Hall's interviews with over 100 people on their reaction to office space revealed that the "single most important criterion is what people can do in the course of their work without bumping into something."[5] Hall concludes that three "hidden zones" exist in American offices.

Zone 1 The work area immediately surrounding the worker, the desktop and chair.

Zone 2 Areas within arm's reach outside zone 1.

Zone 3 Spaces reached by pushing away from the desk without getting up.

Hall found that an "enclosure that permits only movement within the first area is experienced as cramped. An office the size of the second is considered 'small.' An office with Zone 3 space is considered adequate and in some cases ample."[6]

Ergonomics is an interdisciplinary science that studies the relationships between people and their environment. Using human body measurements known as anthropometrics, the ergonomist tries to fit the environment to the user. Because there is no *average user* (so-called average dimensions only mean that in a sampling, 50 percent of the subjects had a specific body measurement and 50 percent did not), a single environment will not satisfy all.

Ideally, office environments should have the flexibility to adjust to varying body measurements and reach limitations, yet most clearance dimensions (the activity/circulation space between objects) are suitable for smaller, but not larger body dimensions. According to a study by Hertzberg, Emanuel, and Alexander, the maximum body breadth was 22.8 inches (not taking into consideration heavy winter clothing or the carrying of briefcases or files), yet many local, state and national codes use 22-inch increments when establishing requirements for corridors, passageways and walkways.[7]

Perhaps because most anthropometric studies in the United States have been conducted by military and aerospace scientists, architects and interior designers have been slow in applying these findings to the civilian environment. In *Human Dimension and Interior Space,* Pannero and Zelnik have translated data into suggested minimum standards for clearances, reach limitations and circulation paths. Every corporation's facility planner should be aware of these dimensions when reconfiguring open plan and enclosed offices or working with architects and designers on the design of new space.

ENTRANCE AND ENCLOSURE

Status within an organization is usually related to how many people and obstacles one needs to pass to gain entrance. Visiting a corporate senior officer is often like visiting the Wizard of Oz. Once past the lobby receptionist, security force and elevators, a visitor is greeted by the floor receptionist, who takes his name a second time and alerts the executive secretary. Stationed so that she can see the visitor approaching (typically the greater her vista, the greater her boss's power), the secretary ushers the visitor to a seating area to await the moment of entrance. If that has not humbled the visitor, passing through the portals will, for the doors will most likely be ceiling-height, of fine wood and custom detailed.

The galleria lounge at AT&T's Long Lines Eastern Region in Oakton (VA) is adrift with fabric sculpture by Karl Rosenberg. It is a dramatic use of space and art for all to enjoy. Interiors by Kohn, Pederson, Fox, Conway with dePolo/Dunbar, Inc. (Photograph by © Ezra Stoller/Esto)

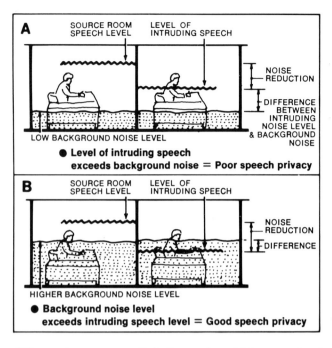

A
SOURCE ROOM SPEECH LEVEL | LEVEL OF INTRUDING SPEECH

NOISE REDUCTION

DIFFERENCE BETWEEN INTRUDING NOISE LEVEL & BACKGROUND NOISE

LOW BACKGROUND NOISE LEVEL

● Level of intruding speech exceeds background noise = Poor speech privacy

B
SOURCE ROOM SPEECH LEVEL | LEVEL OF INTRUDING SPEECH

NOISE REDUCTION
DIFFERENCE

HIGHER BACKGROUND NOISE LEVEL

● Background noise level exceeds intruding speech level = Good speech privacy

(Illustration courtesy Bolt Beranek and Newman Inc.)

Some organizations have an unspoken understanding that doors are almost never shut. In these companies, an open door means you are available; a partially closed door means you would rather not be disturbed.

Moving down the corporate hierarchy, a group secretary replaces the private secretary, the secretary disappears altogether, and then the walls and door disappear.

In an open plan setting, clearly stated ground rules can help employees maintain personal territory. One company, for example, told its employees to treat work station boundaries as walls and doorways. Just as an employee in that company would not enter an enclosed office without an invitation, so he should be invited into a work station area as well. Leaning over partition walls and greeting fellow workers as one passes were also discouraged.

PRIVACY

The need for privacy depends on how information gathering and dissemination takes place. If information is quickly and informally shared, as in a newspaper office or on a trading floor, then privacy is a hindrance. But if information flows through formal channels, the need for privacy is strong.

Sometimes one group will need to share information, but need privacy from others. In a Southwestern insurance company, the personnel department was put in one corner of an open plan floor. High (80-inch) partitions gave the personnel employees visual privacy from one another, but also prevented the easy exchange of information. Soon, confidential personnel data was being shouted over the partitions for all the floor to hear. Turning the partition openings to give the personnel employees eye contact was all that was needed to lower their voices.

According to Franklin Becker in *The Successful Office*, there are two sides of privacy—hearing and being heard and seeing and being seen. Becker feels a workplace should offer three types of privacy:

• **Communication privacy**—where formal and informal information exchanges can occur with a minimum of restrictions.

• **Concentration privacy**—freedom from visual and acoustical distractions.

• **Contemplation privacy**—to reflect on events, plan strategies, or daydream.[8]

Of course, needs will vary depending upon the employee's job tasks. If an employee sees outsiders and clients in his office, communication privacy is a strong need. If creative work is done in the workplace, such as writing a speech or planning a marketing program, concentration privacy is essential. And for those who make decisions, contemplation privacy is a must. Doodling or putting a golf ball may be part of an employee's decision-making process, but others might not view it as "work."

HEARING AND BEING HEARD

A Louis Harris survey (1980) revealed that workers perceived noise as the major problem in their offices. More recently, Michael Brill, head of the Buffalo Organization for Scientific and Technical Innovation (BOSTI), released preliminary findings on a 3-year study of 5000 office workers that emphasized that the need for acoustical privacy was a major factor affecting both productivity and job satisfaction. Jack Curtis, an architect with the acoustics consulting firm of Bolt Beranek and Newman Inc., says that although workers need protection from the sounds of typewriters, copying machines, and telephones, the most distracting noise of all is the sound of other people's conversations.[9]

The extent to which speech is distracting depends primarily on its degree of intelligibility, and its intelligibility depends on how loud the conversation is *as compared to* the background (or ambient) sound in the listener's work area. To provide acoustical privacy the background noise level must be higher than the intruding speech level.[10] It seems ironic, but a quiet office is not the most private.

According to Bolt, Beranek and Newman Inc., absorbing, blocking and covering noise are factors to be considered jointly.

• **Absorbing**—partial height partitions, ceilings and floors should be treated with sound-absorbent materials because hard surfaces reflect sound as a mirror reflects light. Curtains are of little acoustical value.

• **Blocking**—work stations should be arranged so that openings face away from other work stations or hard surfaces such as walls or windows. Because sound waves travel the way light waves do, if workers can see each other, they can hear each other. Large flat-lens lighting fixtures in ceilings also bounce sound from one work area to another. More efficient is up-ambient lighting combined with task lighting as it frees the ceiling from light fixtures altogether.

• **Covering**—raising the level of the background sound is often the least expensive and the most effective. A sound masking system generates an unobtrusive sound—much like an air diffuser—and can be hidden in a suspended ceiling. Portable units are also available, but generally it is best to keep the system (a reminder of the problem) out of sight.

All too often, corporations wait to see how the acoustics will be after they move in and then look for solutions. But that strategy only makes for disgruntled employees and costly and inadequate solutions. Calling in the acoustical consultant at the beginning of the design process can save ill tempers, work disruptions and money.

SEEING AND BEING SEEN

Dr. Jean D. Wineman, professor of architecture at Georgia Institute of Technology, stresses the importance of visual privacy. Several studies (Brookes and Kaplan, 1972; Louis Harris and Associates, 1978; Nemecek and Grandjean, 1973) have found it to be less important than acoustical privacy, but still a strong influence on worker satisfaction. Wineman says that "A lack of visual privacy (privacy from the view of others) may be uncomfortable in and of itself (for example, workers prefer to work side by side than face to face) or may actually interrupt work tasks when passersby stop to initiate conversation."[11] Fortunately, the same work station partitions that block noise can provide visual privacy.

CONTROLLING THE ENVIRONMENT

The employer who perceives himself as having no control over his work area will generally feel he has no control over his work and certainly no control over others. For this reason, some designers are involving their client's staff in certain design choices. The choice could be small—such as do you want a pencil tray or

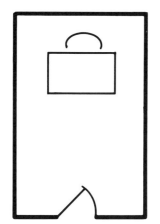

The position of the desk in relation to the door or work station tells others how accessible an employee wishes to be. Facing the door, the employee is most accessible; sitting with his back to the door, he is least accessible; sitting perpendicular to the door is often a good compromise.

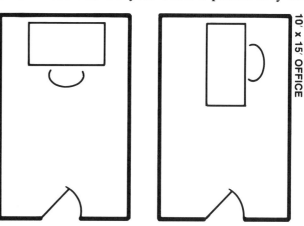

10' x 15' OFFICE

no pencil tray in your drawer? Or on which side of the desk would you like your drawer pedestal? Helping to determine the environment of the company helps the employee to identify with the company.

Just as there is "body language," there is "object language." The positioning of furniture and accessories in a work setting is a strong clue as to how the occupant sees himself and how he wants to be seen. It also signals how much power or control over others he wishes to have and what he considers the boundaries of his territory.

The position of one's desk in relation to the door or work station opening tells others how social or private one wishes to be. A desk facing an entrance is in the least private position—it says that the employee's primary responsibility involves interacting with others. Sitting with one's back to the entrance says just the opposite—this employee does not want to be bothered. Sitting with one's desk perpendicular to the entrance says the employee is approachable and allows privacy as long as the employee can avoid eye contact with passersby.[12]

In a large, enclosed office, the desk is usually positioned as far from the door as possible, yet facing the door to give its occupant maximum power. Approaching the desk is then akin to approaching a throne.

In the broadcasting and recording industries there is a trend towards using no desks. It

Territorial Distance in the Conference Room

	in	cm
A	48–60	121.9–152.4
B	4–6	10.2–15.2
C	20–24	50.8–61.0
D	6–10	15.2–25.4
E	18–24	45.7–61.0
F	30–36	76.2–91.4
G	54–60	137.2–152.4
H	30	76.2
I	72–81	182.9–205.7
J	42–51	106.7–129.5
K	24–27	61.0–68.6
L	48–54	121.9–137.2

(Copyright © 1979, by Julius Panero and Martin Zelnick, reprinted by permission of Whitney Library of Design.)

is doubtful that it will catch on, for the desk and its chair not only serve as a throne when needed, the depth of the desk also serves to set the distance between two people and thus determines the tone for the interchange.

TERRITORIAL DISTANCE

According to Hall, there are four zones of territorial distance: intimate, personal, social and public. Each distance determines how comfortably close or far from others we like to be in a given situation.

• **Intimate distance** extends 1½ feet out from our bodies. This is the distance at which we can easily touch and be touched and is

TERRITORIAL DISTANCES

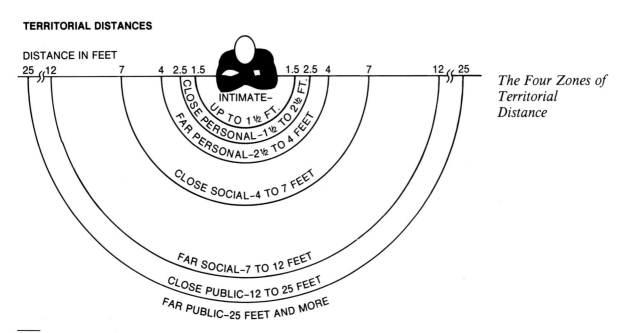

The Four Zones of Territorial Distance

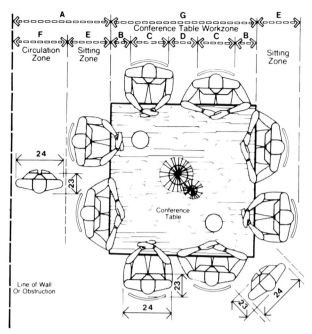

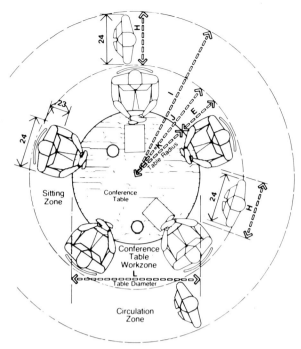

SQUARE CONFERENCE TABLE   CIRCULAR CONFERENCE TABLE

reserved for our most intimate relationships; when others invade this zone, we usually back away.

• **Personal distance** is divided into close—1½ to 2½ feet—and far—2½ to 4 feet—phases. The close phase is still for special relationships; while "keeping someone at arms length" expresses the far phase, and is used for conversations of personal interest and involvements.

• **Social distance** is divided into close—4 to 7 feet—and far—7 to 12 feet—phases. Impersonal business occurs at this distance: the close phase usually reserved for those we work with; the far phase for more formal occasions.

• **Public distance** —the last zone, is well outside the circle of involvement. At the close phase—12 to 25 feet—linguists have observed that a careful choice of words and phrasing occurs as the speaker takes on a "formal style." At the far phase—25 feet or more—the voice is amplified and gestures exaggerated. Thirty feet is the distance instinctively set around important public figures such as a president or royalty.[13]

(These distances generally hold for non-contact middle-class Americans; however, they would not hold for the many cultures whose people like contact, such as Latin Americans, Arabs, and people from southern European countries.)

Knowing these territorial distances exist should be a help in the design of the office, for the advantages and/or restrictions of the setting often determine the tone of the involvement. Therefore, it is not surprising that "tough talks" tend to occur across massive executive desks that insure that the conversants will be seven feet apart—the beginning of far social distance. Or that "friendly" conversations usually take place at closer distances, without fixed barriers; the executive's sofa area, the cafeteria, hallways, and the water fountain are all places where personal distance is possible.

Territorial distance should certainly be considered in the conference room. Conference rooms are often designed to fit the conference table, but what determines the table? Dr. Walter B. Kleeman (*The Challenge of Interior Design*) thinks it is "no accident that the prevailing management theory in America has been predominantly hierarchical until the recent past, and that the conference tables have been rectangular to match."[14] There is an old saying, "At a round table there's no dispute"; however, there is also no head of the table. At a rectangular table, the greater the territorial distance is between the leader and others, the more formal the conference will be.

If a company wants maximum participation in a meeting, the group should be limited to seven or fewer members seated at a round table, 60 inches in diameter. When there are more than seven members, participation be-

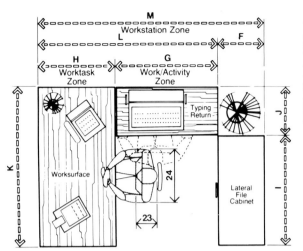

	in	cm
G	46–58	116.8–147.3
H	30–36	76.2–91.4
I	42–50	106.7–127.0
J	18–22	45.7–55.9
K	60–72	152.4–182.9
L	76–94	193.0–238.8
M	94–118	238.8–299.7

BASIC U-SHAPED WORKSTATION

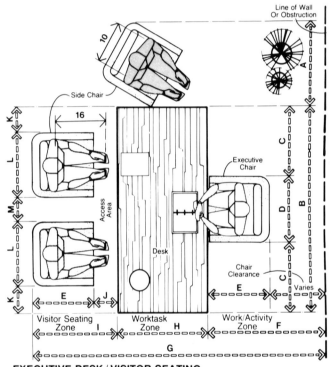

	in	cm
A	30–39	76.2–99.1
B	66–84	167.6–213.4
C	21–28	53.3–71.1
D	24–28	61.0–71.1
E	23–29	58.4–73.7
F	42 min.	106.7 min.
G	105–130	266.7–330.2
H	30–45	76.2–114.3
I	33–43	83.8–109.2
J	10–14	25.4–35.6
K	6–16	15.2–40.6
L	20–26	50.8–66.0
M	12–15	30.5–38.1

EXECUTIVE DESK / VISITOR SEATING

	in	cm
A	96–112	243.8–284.5
B	30–36	76.2–91.4
C	48–54	121.9–137.2
D	18–24	45.7–61.0
E	30	76.2
F	18–22	45.7–55.9
G	29–30	73.7–76.2
H	54–58	137.2–147.3

(Copyright © 1979, by Julius Panero and Martin Zelnick, reprinted by permission of Whitney Library of Design.)

DESK WITH FILING, STORAGE, AND RESTRICTED CIRCULATION

comes concentrated among a few.[15] And, it happens that 66 inches is within the limit for close social distance—the distance people who work together tend to use.

COLOR AND LIGHTING

Lighting is one of the most important aspects of the office environment with both the quality of light and the perceived quality of light important to users. According to Wineman, a 1977 study found that "workers' evaluations of office lighting, and office conditions in general, were influenced by the level of illumination at work stations and such factors as lighting level contrasts and glare."[16]

She also notes that many studies have confirmed that natural lighting is an important factor contributing to environmental satisfaction in offices as it appears to be vital to employees' health and comfort in addition to providing a light source for work. A view reduces perceived crowding, offers contact with the exterior world, and provides visual relief and relaxation. Artificial light, no matter how satisfactory, is unable to provide the variations of color and temperature found in natural light, its soft texture and ambience. But artificial light can extend the benefits of natural light. Wineman says research indicates that if natural light is supplemented by artificial light, workers will overestimate the amount of natural light reaching their work surface and give the entire area a high light quality rating.[17]

Our foreparents worked by the light of a fire, candle, or oil lamp, and later, in 1917, three to six footcandles were considered optimum light for libraries (a footcandle is a unit of measurement for illumination);[18] but recent studies have shown that productivity and accuracy increase with higher levels of illumination.[19] The Illuminating Engineering Society of North America suggests using 10–20 footcandles for corridors, 20–100 for reading and transcribing, to 150 for accounting, and to 200 for designing and drafting.[20]

Faber Birren, the pioneering color consultant, feels it is impossible to separate the effects of light and color. He says that too often lighting engineers forget the factor of appearance—how objects and particularly people's complexions look under light. For instance, cool white fluorescent gives fairly accurate color values, but makes skin tones look palid, while deluxe warm white distorts colors but flatters the complexion. The objections to sodium vapor (yellowish) and clear mercury (greenish) light is based on appearance as well. Although both lights have low energy consumption, and the sodium is an extremely efficient light to work by, people are not enhanced by their tints. The sodium light, for instance, washes out the reds of women's makeup, while the mercury light turns complexions greenish and lips black. Neither are morale boosters.[21]

In natural daylight, color is warm at sunrise, cool at noon, and warm again at sunset, with brightness increasing toward noon and then receding again toward sunset. Through all of these changes, colors are true because the warm light of sunrise and sunset gives a normal color appearance when light levels are low, while the cool light of midday gives a natural appearance with bright light levels. Some lamp manufacturers are aware of this and specify low light levels for warm lights and high light levels for cool ones.[22]

Therefore, Birren suggests we use more than one type of light and level in our buildings: low-level warm in rest areas, higher-level warm for food service, cooler and still higher for working areas. Lighting which allows for highlights and shadows, subtle shifts in color tint, and reductions in flatness and monotony would be more like nature's own and thus more desirable.[23]

Birren says it "is fallacious to assume that because color is appealing and attractive, it is conducive to enjoyable labor. Indeed, for the very reason of its strong impact, it may, when not properly applied, distract from work, interfere with tasks, and actually make seeing difficult and fatiguing."[24] Reflection and contrast are the culprits: a white desk, for instance, may bounce glare up into the eyes and constrict the pupil opening; a black or dark desk will appear too great a contrast to papers and other objects. Both will result in eye fatigue.

Recommended reflectances for surfaces

range from 20 percent for floors, to 25–40 percent for furniture, to 40–60 percent for walls, to 80–90 percent for ceilings. For contrast, certain walls could be in the 25–40 percent range.)[25] Translated, this means colors get progressively lighter from the floor up. Using grey as an example, one might have a medium-to-dark grey carpet, a medium grey desk, pale grey walls and a white ceiling, with one wall darker for contrast.

Color and brightness can also produce emotional and psychological effects: "Where there is high brightness and warm color, attention will extend outward to an environment, and this reaction may be favorable for the performance of muscular tasks. On the other hand, where there is lower brightness and cooler color, the environment will be less distracting, human attention will be directed inward, and the reaction here will be favorable for more exacting visual and mental tasks."[26]

The importance of color and lighting in business interiors cannot be stressed enough. Every other element of a space might be right, but if color and lighting are wrong, everything seems wrong. The problem is that they are both a science and an art; both objective and subjective reactions must be considered.

When creating working environments, we must start by observing the worker and determining his needs. Copying another company's solutions will not do. Neither will handing the job over to an architect or designer and leaving it at that. Since all individuals are unique, their sum will produce a unique company as well. Corporate design is making that unique company quality visible.

A typical "American plan office" in the early 1900s at Chicago's Monadnock Building, designed by Holabird & Roche, 1892. (Photograph courtesy of "The Montauk Co.," the current owner/manager of the building)

An original office in The Monadnock Building. Note the residential ambience created by the painting, roll-top desk and oriental carpet. (Photograph courtesy of "The Montauk Co.")

An original outer office in The Monadnock Building. Note the frosted glass partitions which were typical in this period. (Photograph courtesy of "The Montauk Co.")

A BRIEF HISTORY OF THE OFFICE

Offices moved outside the home during the Industrial Revolution of the late 18th and 19th centuries, and brought with them the ambiance of the private study. In the mid-1800s, office buildings in America were, as many European offices still are, a series of small windowed rooms along a corridor that companies rented as needed. This meant that sometimes a firm's offices were not adjacent, but spaced out along the corridor with other firms in between. Typically, the head of the firm had one private office with a clerk on the other side of a frosted or stained-glass partition. Other staff members were situated in other rooms, which were usually just open spaces with desks. Oil or gas lamps supplemented natural light; heat was supplied by stoves and fireplaces. Oriental rugs, roll-top desks and leather chairs were standard office furnishings.

Several inventions sped the development of office technology in the 19th century: the Morse telegraph (introduced to the public in 1844), the pencil eraser (followed by the ink and typewriter erasers) in 1858, the typewriter in 1868, and the telephone in 1876.

By the beginning of the 20th century, buildings of steel and iron provided a new type of office inspired by the factories—whole floors were open, broken only by cast-iron columns, with row upon row of desks. The spaces were long and narrow, with high ceilings to accommodate tall windows and provide proper ventilation. Electricity was used to supplement daylight.

And women were suddenly on the scene

Chicago's Old Colony Building was designed by Holabird & Roche in 1894. (Photograph and floor plan courtesy of Old Colony Building, a Murdoch & Coll property, Chicago)

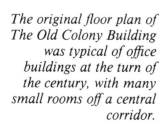

The original floor plan of The Old Colony Building was typical of office buildings at the turn of the century, with many small rooms off a central corridor.

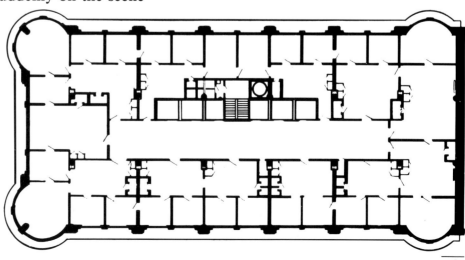

This Southeastern insurance company office was typical of smaller "American plan offices" of the 1920s—one large room containing many desks and the newly introduced file cabinets. Electricity now supplemented natural light and women moved into the offices in force to operate the typewriters and telephones. (Photograph courtesy of Integon Corporation)

During World War II, women took over many office duties when their male co-workers went overseas. Here, insurance employees work in desk-to-desk rows. (Photograph courtesy of Integon Corporation)

in force—to operate the telephones and typewriters—in these "American plan offices" (as the Europeans dubbed them). Large organizations such as mail-order houses, insurance companies and government agencies sometimes contained hundreds of clerical workers, with managers in a private office nearby and the executives usually far removed. Double pedestal desks and sturdy, slat-back chairs of oak became the norm. Wooden filing cabinets to hold the accumulating paperwork were introduced. Offices became "organized" and lost their homey touches. In the 1920s, some offices went modern and switched to steel furniture and files.

During the 1940s, office furniture was predominately "period" in style. If an architect wanted functional, modern furnishings, he had to either design it himself or turn to a handful of contemporary furniture manufacturers such as Knoll, Herman Miller and Thonet. These companies made furniture designed by architects—classics which are now in museum collections. Mies van der Rohe's Barcelona and Brno chairs, the molded plywood furniture of Charles and Ray Eames, Eero Saarinen's molded fiberglass seating, Harry Bertoia's wire furniture and Marcel Breuer's tubular-steel chairs, were a few of the famous early designs. Modular office furniture and wall storage systems also appeared in the early 1940s.

Advances in heating, ventilating, air conditioning and lighting technologies after World War II and the invention of the first electronic computer, INIAC, in 1946, changed the look of offices again. During the 1950s and 1960s, the "conventional" office became popular as multinational corporations commissioned International Style, block-square skyscrapers with interiors that reflected the hierarchical structure of management. Space planners (a new professional) used the dimensions of the exterior building module to plan the interiors.

The result was a grid design that integrated all elements—ceiling, partitions, desks—and allowed the offices to be precisely sized and graded according to an employee's rank. The top people were then assigned the largest offices, on the highest floors, with the

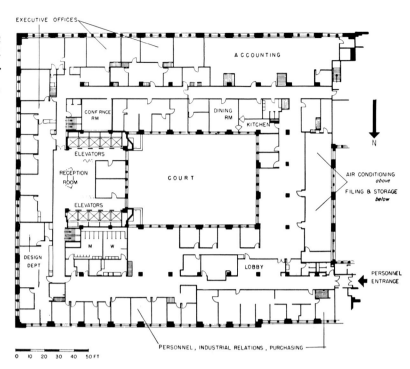

Floor plan of Container Corporation of America shows many enclosed offices, most of which have exterior or central court windows.

EXECUTIVE OFFICES

ACCOUNTING

CONF RNCE RM

DINING RM

KITCHEN

ELEVATORS

RECEPTION ROOM

COURT

AIR CONDITIONING *above*

FILING & STORAGE *below*

ELEVATORS

M   W

DESIGN DEPT

LOBBY

PERSONNEL ENTRANCE

0 10 20 30 40 50 FT

PERSONNEL, INDUSTRIAL RELATIONS, PURCHASING

In 1948, the Container Corporation of America moved into a hot and noisy older office building in downtown Chicago. Its solution was to seal the windows, lower the ceilings, and air condition the entire area. The furniture and most of the executive offices were designed by Maria Bergson working in collaboration with Herbert Bayer, colorist, and Morton L. Pereira & Associates, architects. (Photograph by the Hedrich-Blessing Studio)

In 1950, the New York City offices of Time & Life were remodeled by Maria Bergson. In the company's Travel Bureau, wall-to-wall carpeting and the acoustical treatment of ceilings, screens and bookcase backs helped to mute conversations and office noise. (Photograph by Robert Damora)

best views; while the majority of workers received small, windowless offices or bull-pen situations on the interior. Although the movable partitions could be rearranged, the reality was that moving one was almost as disruptive as moving a permanent wall. Other disadvantages of the conventional office were the absence of operable windows and the extensive use of fluorescent ceiling fixtures which made these buildings expensive to operate later in the 1970s and 1980s.

The colors of the conventional office were white spiked with the primaries—red, blue and yellow. These colors, combined with the grid design, were often reminiscent of a Mondrian painting. Noteworthy early examples were the Union Carbide headquarters in New York, and the Connecticut General headquarters in Bloomfield (CT) designed by Skidmore, Owings & Merrill with the Knoll Planning Unit doing the interiors; and Time, Inc. designed by Gerald Luss and Designs for Business in New York.

Although built in 1939, Frank Lloyd Wright's administration building for S.C. Johnson & Son in Racine, Wisconsin, bridged the gap between the conventional office and the next development—office landscaping. Still in use today, the Great Workroom at Johnson Wax is 128 by 208 feet with interior columns reaching more than 21 feet up to a glass roof. Clerical employees fill the central

A noteworthy early example of the "conventional office" was the Union Carbide headquarters in New York, constructed in 1959. Reflecting the hierarchical structure of management, the private offices were ringed around the building's exterior and sized according to an employee's rank. The support staff was located in the interior sections. Skidmore, Owings & Merrill was the architect; the Knoll Planning Unit did the interiors. (Photograph by Joseph W. Molitor)

OPPOSITE
Two views of an executive office in the Union Carbide Building, 1959. (Photographs courtesy of Union Carbide Corporation)

section of this light-filled room with managers occupying the two-tiered perimeter. Although there are no partitions between workers, there is plenty of space. The furniture was designed in collaboration with the manufacturer, Steelcase, to make work more efficient and comfortable—swing-out bins were used rather than drawers, a shelf was added above the work surface, and the upholstered chair had a tilting back. To integrate the furniture with the design of the building, Wright painted the metal brick red and curved the forms.

Office Landscaping, or open plan design, as it is commonly called, had its origins in Germany around 1958 when a management consulting group, the Quickborner Team für Planung und Organisation, concluded that the typical existing office hindered rather than encouraged work productivity. Joining forces

with a space planner, the Quickborner Team eliminated partitions and thus, the enclosed office, the geometric grid and space modules.

Instead, they wanted to plan in a "green field"—a large, unpartitioned room where, ideally, more than 100 employees would be given work stations and grouped according to communication needs. Space and privacy requirements were to be evaluated and only real needs provided for. The Quickborner Team suggested that files be in a central location with open file carts used at the workplace, all furniture and screens be light in weight and easy to move, and that lighting, acoustics, temperature and humidity be uniformly ideal throughout the room.[27]

Key to the Quickborner plan was a communication survey whereby employees kept a log to discover the real lines of interaction

In 1967, DuPont asked the Quickborner Team to design one floor of its Wilmington (DE) headquarters using open landscape design. None of DuPont's managers chose to adopt the test space approach in their own sections. (Photograph courtesy of Quickborner Team)

within the organization. Although such surveys are commonplace today, at the time it was a revolutionary idea and it threatened the conventional organization structure which isolated top management and separated middle managers from their subordinates.

Because the Quickborner Team did away with enclosed offices for everyone—including top executives—it was difficult to elicit management's enthusiasm for "Bürolandschaft," or office landscape design in the United States.

Also, one look at American cities clearly illustrates our national love of the grid and explains why Americans are often confused in foreign cities which are not based on the grid. (A "grid" design is based on right angles.) Although the Quickborner Team felt random patterning was necessary to be both more

responsive to organizational relationships and avoid monotony, Americans resisted the unstructured design.

Quite independent of Quickborner, Robert Probst of Herman Miller developed the Action Office in 1960—the first commercially successful system of office components which could stand on legs or be attached to panels. The system could be highly individualized; if needed, a worker could have both standard seating and a high stool for perching.

John Pile, in *Open Office Planning,* says that by combining the office landscape concept and the Action Office furniture, Americans were able to overcome many of their previous objections. The Action Office provided more storage than the pure German model, and its panels offered much more privacy.[28]

Many manufacturers developed their

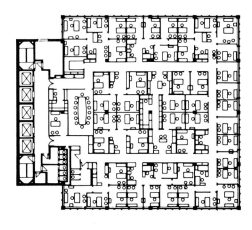
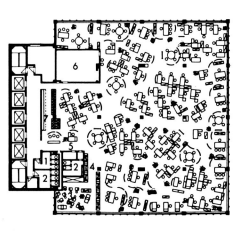

The floor plan of a "conventional office" floor at DuPont, and one of the open landscape test floor.

own systems inspired by Action Office, while others, such as Knoll, designed a heavier-weight system of wood that more closely resembled conventional office furniture. Called the Stephens System, it was originally designed by Knoll for the Weyerhaeuser Corporation in Seattle.

Corporations today often mix the different office types in one facility. The general office areas may be open plan with managers in open or enclosed offices; upper management may receive enclosed offices with size and furniture determined by precise office standards; while the chairman and president may be surrounded by antiques and/or custom furnishings, all the ambience of home, and more. There are no absolutes in corporate design. Whatever supports your company's work needs and desired image is absolutely right.

Frank Lloyd Wright integrated the furniture with the design of the Johnson Wax building by painting the metal brick red and curving the forms. To make work easier and more comfortable, Wright used swing-out bins for drawers, designed additional storage levels above and below the worksurface, and gave the chair a tilting back. (Photograph courtesy of Steelcase)

The Great Workroom at Johnson Wax (S.C. Johnson & Son) in Racine (WI) was designed by Frank Lloyd Wright in 1939 and is still in use today. Managers occupy the two-tiered perimeter of the space, while clerical employees fill the central section. (Photograph courtesy of Johnson Wax)

ENTRANCE AND RECEPTION

The corporation's image is born at the entrance and reception area. Here is the first contact with a company employee—the receptionist and possibly the security staff. It is a space that must at once welcome and guard for it is the one area that all visitors will see, be they bank presidents, messengers or intruders.

Since the area must be relatively large to receive such diverse traffic, it can also be the one monumental or formal space in the facility. Yet its plan must be obvious and signage should be visable and distinctive.

The reception desk is the key, as it must work for both the seated receptionist and the standing visitor. It should not leave the receptionist vulnerable, yet its depth must allow for the exchange of packages and envelopes.

Sometimes visitors must wait. Individual seating just this side of comfortable works best here for the business of this space is circulation—moving on.

Visitors to the Dallas headquarters of Scor Re, a French reinsurance firm, enter a stylish reception area where a granite floor and glass ceiling reflect an illusion of greater space; the design is by PLM Design. Dai Tokyo Insurance presented the bell on the pedestal. (Photograph by Mark Ross)

Since International Paper makes forest products, the executive reception at its New York headquarters is a showcase for wood: oak columns, teak floor, tamo desk, and tamo and zebra paneling. The designer is The Space Design Group. (Photograph by Mark Ross)

OPPOSITE
A glass pavilion contains the reception area of Banco de la Nacion Argentina for privacy without confinement. The Miami office was designed by Interspace, Inc. (Photograph by Dan Forer)

Veined marble, oak cornices and dramatic up lighting give monumentality to the reception area of Rozansky and Kay Construction in Bethesda (MD), designed by Deupi and Associates. (Photograph by Ron Solomon/Eileen Brown © 1982)

OPPOSITE
Sidney Philip Gilbert designed this reception area for Ramco (now Nico), New York general contractors, to show clients skilled work like the arched doorway, custom cabinetry and stairway to the executive floor. The photography is by Berenice Abbott. (Photograph by © Peter Aaron/Esto)

The sculptural entrance to Georgia Power Company headquarters in Atlanta, designed by Heery & Heery, is approached by visitors on the mezzanine and by employees on the lower level; the reception desk is on the left. (Photograph by Paul G. Beswick)

Soft light behind a glass block wall and furnishings with softly rounded contours create a soothing ambience in a Miami office designed by Robison and Associates. (Photograph by Steven Brooke)

A 1911 tower frames the entrance to Meredith Corp., publisher of Better Homes and Gardens, *Des Moines. A Richard Haas trompe l'oeil mural extends its vistas. The designer was Charles Herbert and Associates. (Photograph by Architectural Fotographics/Paul S. Kivett)*

Alert visitors to the offices designed by Arquitectonica for The Overseas Group, a diversified holding company, will observe that the reception area is a scale model of the Miami building housing it. (Photograph by Timothy Hursley © The Arkansas Office)

The reception area in Warner Bros. headquarters in Burbank (CA) plays pale colors against dhurrie rugs and enlargements from classic films such as Casablanca *(1942) that command attention. The designer was The Luckman Partnership, Inc. and Swimmer, Cole, Martinez, Curtis (Photograph by Toshi Yoshimi)*

An appropriate greeting awaits affluent customers of U.S. Trust Co. in the reception hall of a historic New York townhouse renovated by Haines, Lundberg, Waehler. (Photograph by George Cserna)

OPPOSITE
The reception area for the corporate law firm of Spears, Lubersky, Campbell and Bledsoe, Portland, is dignified by fine proportions, rich materials and stately columns, designed by Gensler and Associates. (Photograph by Jaime Ardiles-Arce)

Symmetry and traditional and modern furnishings establish a formal reception area for financial officers visiting INA/CIGNA's investment management offices in Philadelphia, designed by Venturi, Rauch and Scott Brown. (Photograph by Tom Bernard)

Gensler and Associates Architects modified an old San Francisco warehouse for Young & Rubicam, leaving most surfaces pure white and adding bright color for vitality. Here the reception area is a distinct first stop for visitors. (Photograph by Jaime Ardiles-Arce)

CONFERENCE ROOMS

Corporate policies are created, contracts negotiated, deals sealed, reports given and glasses risen in conference rooms. When it is a board room, it is usually on a grand scale—suitable for pomp and circumstance and important meetings. For many firms, the conference room must represent the entire facility as it is one of the few rooms outsiders will be shown, other than the reception area. In Europe and Japan it is the only room seen.

The table determines the shape of the room and the tone of the meeting. Livelier meetings take place in tighter quarters. Full participation work meetings are thus most effective with seven or fewer members seated at a 60-inch round table. The greater the stress, the more space is needed. The space between participants at large tables insures formality and uneven participation. Large tables also define hierarchy—particularly the rectangle. It becomes a question of matching management style and purpose to table shape.

Site lines and acoustics can be a problem. Chairs that swivel and speaker systems are a help. Good ventilation is a must. Since the conference room is often used for formal dining, a kitchen and restrooms nearby are necessary.

Technology in conference rooms is a tool and status symbol; teleconferencing is the latest. The question here is one of control—who should pull the switches? The technicians or the executives? And what should they control?—security, draperies, lighting, the A/V?

At the Rozansky & Kay Construction Company in Washington (DC), the conference room is used several hours each day for audio/visual presentations, large meetings and formal lunches prepared by a fulltime cook in the adjoining executive kitchen. Deupi and Associates designed the room around a massive rosso alicante *marble table. It is an impressive, substantial look aimed at making visiting bankers feel right at home. (Photograph by Ron Solomon/Eileen Brown © 1982)*

Because Genstar Corporation, a diversified Canadian industrial company in San Francisco, has two CEOs, Environmental Planning and Research placed two chairs at the head of its conference table with a console in between to control lighting, audio/visual aids, drapes and entry doors. Teleconferencing allows the California executives to "meet" regularly with their Canadian counterparts. (Photograph by © Peter Aaron/Esto)

OPPOSITE
The board room and adjoining executive lounge at AT&T's Long Lines Eastern Region Headquarters in Oakton (VA) shows contemporary elegance with a lacquered and brass table, leather chairs and fine wood paneling. The interiors were designed by Kohn, Pederson, Fox in joint venture with dePolo/Dunbar Inc. The painting in the executive lounge is by Wolf Kahn, part of a corporate art program assembled by art consultant Marilyn Falk. (Photograph by © Ezra Stoller/Esto)

Diamond Shamrock's Industrial Chemicals Group in Dallas has a glass wall to maintain acoustical privacy while sharing the city skyline view. Harwood K. Smith & Partners designed the company logo into custom carpeting, using it throughout the completely open plan facility. (Photograph by © Greg Hursley)

Ramco (now Nico), a general contractor specializing in the construction of space, wanted its own New York City offices to display its talents. Although the space was quite modest, Sidney Philip Gilbert & Associates' design created an illusion of generous size with glass, geometry and lighting; details such as the piano-hinged, arched doors underscore the importance of the conference room. (Photograph by Norman McGrath)

Southwest Forest Industries, a forest product company in Phoenix (AZ), chose a board room table of cherry with an inset of brass. Designed by Peter A. Lendrum Associates/Interior Architecture Division, the room has a glass interior wall with a floating bronze chair rail to take advantage of the views on the other side of the building. Double draperies are concealed in the book-matched cherry wall paneling for use when privacy is desired. Plush leather chairs are comfortable no matter how long the meeting. (Photograph by Al Payne © 1981)

OPPOSITE

The board room table at Oak Industries, an electronics company, is made up of individual tables, each with its own floor lamp. The hacienda-style headquarters in Rancho Bernardo (CA), designed by Dale Naegle Architecture and Planning Inc. with interiors by Brenda Mason Design Associates, has Mexican colonial motifs such as exposed wood beams, burnished plaster walls, and cast stone fireplaces throughout. (Photograph by Charles Schneider)

OPPOSITE

Alusuisse of America, a Swiss holding company, located in I.M. Pei's gleaming black tower, 499 Park Avenue in New York, wanted its board room to have a softer feeling than the rest of its space. Samuel De Santo provided a leather table edged with black stained wood and fabric upholstered chairs. The central ceiling strip houses incandescent lighting with diffusers; power wedge louvres, with fluorescent lighting flank each side. (Photograph by Mark Ross)

Frank O. Gehry & Associates' design for Mid-Atlantic Toyota, a distributor in Glen Burnie (MD), uses corrugated metal siding, industrial carpet, and a ceiling that exposes the mechanical and electrical systems to create a simple, yet handsome, setting for a conference room. (Photograph by Ron Solomon)

The board room at Best Products, catalog showroom merchandisers in Richmond, could easily win a "most unusual" award. Designed by Hardy Holzman Pfeiffer Associates, the room has a most interesting wood inlay table. The curving end of the table is inset with glass and lit from below. (Photograph by Norman McGrath)

76

At Georgia Power, a utility company in Atlanta (GA), a semi-open conference room was constructed after move-in to give the personnel department additional meeting space. Designed by Heery Interiors, Inc., the area behind the conference module is a lounge used by the adjacent training rooms for breaks. (Photograph by Timothy Hursley © The Arkansas Office)

CENTER

The Gulf State Utilities Company in Beaumont (TX) wanted to avoid ostentatious design; Morris/ Aubry Architects suggested clean lines with architectural interest. The stepped wall treatment, column, and wall sconces are examples in the board room. (Photograph by chas mcgrath)

BOTTOM

The conference/hearing room at the offices of the Bar Counsel in Boston conveys an aura of ceremony with a column in each corner and a large table which is actually four. The designer, Charles G. Hilgenhurst Associates Inc., furnished the room with two entrances to assure lawyers' privacy when attending hearings. (Photograph by Herb Engelsburg © 1980)

OPPOSITE ABOVE
Scor Re, a French reinsurance firm in Dallas, chose a circular table for its sophisticated board room designed by PLM Design, Inc. One clear glass wall overlooks the lobby and stairs. (Photograph by Mark Ross)

OPPOSITE BELOW
Adam Tihany designed the offices for Intermarco Advertising in New York City. Most furniture and all cabinetry is custom designed of curly maple with a hand-rubbed lacquer finish and black lacquer detail. (Photograph by Mark Ross)

ABOVE
The investment operations of INA/CIGNA in Philadelphia required offices that are modern yet traditional in spirit. Venturi, Rauch and Scott Brown, architects, featured fine fabrics and architectural woodworking. (Photograph by Tom Bernard)

RIGHT
The larger of two conference rooms at the American Academy of Arts and Sciences in Brookline (MA) has a descending ceiling that is the primary light source. The architecture is by Kallman, McKinnell, McKinnell & Wood, with ISD as interior design consultants. (Photograph by Jaime Ardiles-Arce)

EXECUTIVE OFFICES

EXECUTIVE OFFICES

No matter how "comfortable" an executive office, there is always the knowledge that herein resides a person of influence. For visitors, the executive office is symbolic of the corporation's power; for employees it is a goal to strive for; and for the executive, it is the reward for service beyond the call. Luxury is expected—it is the norm.

And it is intimidating, as it should be; there are times when the executive needs this shield of power—this show of strength. And then, just as an Army sergeant puts his officers at ease, so the executive puts his visitors at ease—in his lounge area.

For strength, the most important component in the executive office is the desk itself and the objects related to it, such as the chair, the storage unit and accessories. The deeper the desk, the more formal the conversation across it will be. The higher and plusher the chair, the more throne-like it seems. Some executives put their visitors in chairs with lower seats (denoting lower status?), or seats that are uncomfortable, or difficult to move or get up from, while the executive tilts and swivels and controls in comfort.

Gensler and Associates slanted walls at 45 degrees to encompass an ocean view and block off downtown in the president's office at Wilshire Associates, financial advisers, Santa Monica (CA). Built-in bookshelves and a sectional seating group surround the desk, creating a private space within the larger room. (Photograph by Jaime Ardiles-Arce)

A pair of neo-Georgian townhouses in New York designed for James J. Goodwin in 1896 by McKim, Mead & White has been restored as bank offices for U.S. Trust Co. by Haines, Lundberg, Waehler.

The former living room houses several senior officers. Sconces and the chandelier are reproductions. Another former parlor now used by an officer features mahogany woodwork and an Agra Persian carpet, circa 1900. (Photographs by George Cserna)

A desire for a relaxed atmosphere and hands-on management is shown in the president's office at Arco Metals, Rolling Meadows (IL), designed by Lee Manners & Assoc. (Photograph by © Peter Aaron/Esto)

Mexican art motifs against modern furniture impart special flavor to the president's office at Bufete Industrial, engineering and industrial giant, Mexico City. The designers were Juan José Diaz-Infante and The Display Center. (Photograph by Timothy Hursley, © The Arkansas Office)

Art objects reflect the special interests of the executive vice president of Best Products, catalog showroom merchandisers, at Richmond (VA) headquarters designed by Hardy, Holzman, Pfeiffer. (Photograph by Norman McGrath)

OPPOSITE

The San Francisco offices of the president and chairman of Genstar, a diversified Canadian industrial company, are appointed in antiques and traditional furniture for propriety and comfort. Panoramic views from the windows sweep from the Bay Bridge to the Golden Gate. The designer is Environmental Planning and Research. (Photograph by © Peter Aaron/Esto)

The chairman's office of International Paper in New York, designed by The Space Design Group, displays a collection of handcrafted wood furniture by George Nakashima. Wood is used as a design motif throughout the offices. (Photograph by Mark Ross)

ABOVE
A scenic view of Dallas, 15-foot ceilings and stylish lacquered furnishings call attention to the president of Scor Re, a French reinsurance firm designed by PLM. (Photograph by Mark Ross)

For the Long Beach (CA) office of the president of Van de Kamp's, food processors, Swimmer, Cole, Martinez, Curtis relaxed the severe Bauhaus style. (Photograph by Sheldon Lettich)

OPPOSITE
The president's office at Sperry and Hutchinson, New York, was designed by Kirk White, the company's director of design. (Photograph by Jaime Ardiles-Arce)

Cherry furniture and birch doors add warmth to the president's office at Southwest Forest Industries, Phoenix, designed by Metz, Train & Youngren and Peter A. Lendrum Associates/Interior Architecture. The woods are marketed by the company. (Photograph by Al Payne © 1981)

To emphasize superb views of Biscayne Bay, Miami, Interspace combined a beige and blue color scheme with reflective ceilings in the general manager's office at Banco de la Nacion Argentina. (Photograph by Dan Forer)

Modern office technology is discreetly integrated in a traditional executive office at INA/CIGNA's investment management firm in Philadelphia by Venturi, Rauch and Scott Brown. (Photograph by Tom Bernard)

Shifting the president's desk and seating 45 degrees made his office at Ramco (now Nico), a New York general contractor, seem more generous. The designer was Sidney Philip Gilbert & Associates. (Photograph by Norman McGrath)

A high technology image is for the chairman at USA Today, Gannett's national newspaper, Rosslyn (VA), designed by Environmental Planning and Research. Satellite transmissions to printing plants make the map flash on. (Photograph by © Peter Aaron/Esto)

Restored classical paneling is played off sleek modern furniture and accent lighting in the executive office of Edward J. Safdie in New York. The designer was Charles Swerz and Assoc. (Photograph by Mark Ross)

The partners of Rozansky & Kay Construction, Bethesda (MD), divide their activities between design, construction and engineering (BELOW) and acquisition, finance and management (TOP), as contemporary and traditional styles by Deupi and Associates suggest. (Photograph by Ron Solomon/Eileen Brown © 1982)

A simple yet elegant office for the managing partner of Maloney, Chase, Fisher & Hurst, attorneys, frames a view of three San Francisco bridges. The designer was Tardy and Associates. (Photograph by Russell Abraham)

Working with very distinctive furnishings, Warren Hansen and Maitland/Strauss/Behr Associates designed a whimsical New York townhouse office for the leader of the Muppets. (Photograph by Jaime Ardiles-Arce)

No walls enclose the president or anyone else at Diamond Shamrock Industrial Chemicals, Dallas, designed by Harwood K. Smith & Partners. The open area is defined by furnishings. (Photograph by © Greg Hursley)

Authentic Mexican colonial motifs were used in the chairman's office and throughout Oak Industries headquarters, Rancho Bernardo (CA), to blend with the surroundings. The designers were Dale Naegle and Brenda Mason Design Associates. (Photograph by Charles Schneider)

From the president's office at Integon, the Winston-Salem insurance subsidiary of Ashland Oil, one can see across a balcony as far north as Virginia. Inside, flame-stitch upholstery on traditional chairs is the focal point for a contemporary interior in orange, beige, blue and cherry veneer. The designer was Welton Becket, Chicago. (Photograph by Mark Ross)

EXECUTIVE BATHS

The rich materials used in executive baths—such as wood, stone, stainless steel—combined with the use of low level, dramatic lighting creates not a utilitarian restroom, but rather a vestment room. A room where the executive can go to compose himself, to see himself not critically, but how he would like to be seen.

There is an ambience of the home here—a linen closet, toiletries, a shower, usually a bed or cot, and frequently exercise apparatus. It is symbolic of status, to be sure, but it seems also a concession to the long hours the executive puts in. It is a private place, a small piece of home away from home.

Having one's own bathroom means not having to use the general restroom and run the chance of being trapped by the rank and file. Press conferences are better held under more formal circumstances.

The Space Design Group created private washrooms entered from a separate foyer for executives at International Paper headquarters in New York. (Photograph by Mark Ross)

Black granite, a nickel silver basin and custom faucet handles are reflected in the New York executive bath designed by Skidmore, Owings & Merrill, San Francisco, for GFI/Knoll, an industrial company. (Photograph by Jaime Ardiles-Arce)

Modern cabinetry, a barber chair and stainless steel fixtures create a very contemporary executive bath for one of two partners at Rozansky & Kay Construction, Bethesda (MD), designed by Deupi and Associates. This partner is responsible for construction and design.

A very traditional bath is preferred by the other partner, whose duties include finance and administration. Here Deupi used architectural paneling, brass fixtures and marble. (Photographs by Ron Solomon/ Eileen Brown © 1982)

For what appears to be the compleat executive in New York, Eric Bernard has designed a bath that combines bath, physical fitness, telecommunications center and valet storage. (Photograph by Peter Paige)

Black lacquer, stainless steel and recessed down lighting produce an urbane and luxurious bath for a private investor in Washington, DC. The designer was dePolo/Dunbar. (Photograph by © Peter Aaron/Esto)

EXECUTIVE DINING

Sometimes a conference room is used for executive dining, but more frequently a graciously scaled room is set aside for this most important ritual—the breaking of bread. Whether the purpose is to entertain a visitor or get to know another executive within the company better, there is a definite aura of ceremony to this room.

Again, the expensive materials and residential feeling make a statement—the rich woods, fine linen and silver tell executives that dining here is a very special privilege—a sign of favor—they are now part of the "family."

Often, the views from this room are the best in the building. Many executive dining rooms have an adjacent lounge for cocktails before the meal. A kitchen should be adjacent also, or at least nearby. Some corporations have full-time cooks on staff, others have meals catered and use the kitchen primarily for serving. Buffet self-service is often the style in large dining rooms, while smaller, more formal rooms provide table service.

One section of the board room at Sutro & Co., a San Francisco brokerage house, is adjacent to a full kitchen so it can be closed off for dining. A Japanese screen complements the garden view. The designer was Gensler and Associates. (Photograph by Jaime Ardiles-Arce)

This dining room is one of two that can be opened or closed to a central atrium at the American Academy of Arts and Sciences in Cambridge (MA) by Kallman, McKinnell & Wood with Louis Beal and Joseph Rosen of ISD. (Photograph by Jaime Ardiles-Arce)

A country location is portrayed with weather vanes and a grain sifter in the executive dining room at ARCO Chemical and Engineering Research Center, Philadelphia, designed by Llewelyn Davies Associates, Davis Brody Associates and Kenneth Parker Associates. (Photograph by Tom Crane)

Warm personal relationships are sustained with traditional furnishings used by Juan José Diaz-Infante and The Display Center for Bufete Industrial, an engineering and construction firm in Mexico City. (Photograph by Timothy Hursley © The Arkansas Office)

Small tables and lounge seating foster a relaxed feeling in the directors' dining room of Braniff's Dallas/Fort Worth headquarters by Morris-Aubry. (Photograph by Jaime Ardiles-Arce)

A separate dining room is provided for the chairman of International Paper at New York headquarters featuring woodcraft by George Nakashima and a Robert Motherwell lithograph. A detail of the dining table shows the American walnut slab selected by Nakashima. The designer was The Space Design Group. (Photograph by Mark Ross)

The view of San Francisco from the executive dining room of Genstar, a diversified Canadian industrial, is its showpiece in a design by Environmental Planning and Research. (Photograph by © Peter Aaron/ Esto)

A quiet setting is provided for executive dining with neutral colors and soft lighting at Georgia Power, Atlanta, designed by Heery & Heery. (Photograph by Paul G. Beswick)

OPPOSITE
The dining room is part of the president's suite, used to receive important clients at Flagship Bank, Miami, designed by Hellmuth, Obata & Kassabaum, Dallas. (Photograph by Yuichi Idaka)

*Built-in cabinetry and a credenza transform the confer-
ence room of the Edward J. Safdie Group, New York,
into executive dining. Charles Swerz and Assoc. was
the designer. (Photograph by Mark Ross)*

*A pale color scheme is offset by colorful wall tapestries
at Anaconda headquarters in Denver by Neville Lewis
Associates and Kaneko-Laff Associates. (Photograph
by Jaime Ardiles-Arce)*

Japanese craftsmen built a tea room for Mid-Atlantic Toyota, Glen Burnie (MD), designed by Frank O. Gehry and Associates. (Photograph by Ron Solomon)

An 18th-century New England farmhouse room has served J. Walter Thompson, the advertising giant, as executive dining for five decades. The designer was Griswold, Heckel & Kelly. (Photo courtesy of JWT)

In Rosslyn (VA), con-
trasting finishes, built-in
storage, recessed lighting
and modern furniture
make for sophisticated
executive dining rooms
for USA Today, Gan-
nett's national newspa-
per. The designer was
Environmental Planning
and Research. (Photo-
graph by © Peter Aaron/
Esto)

OPPOSITE
The main dining room
of Reliance Group Hold-
ings, New York, uses
marble, slate and oak for
a solid, business appear-
ance. Gwathmey Siegel
& Associates was the de-
signer. (Photograph by
Jaime Ardiles-Arce)

CAFETERIAS

Every day close to 20 million employees in the United States eat in their company cafeterias and dining rooms. And as more corporations move to areas without restaurants and many employees find restaurants "too expensive," the demand for employee food service is increasing.

Typically, the cafeteria is a spacious room that gives workers a change of scene and a chance to behave more informally than in the office. It allows employees to get officially away from their work to a place with brighter colors, plants and art—a comfortable, upbeat ambience. Often, an employee lounge is near the cafeteria.

Although some cafeterias still have an institutional image, most are striving for a restaurant image with tables of various sizes and groupings. Some companies have designated "no smoking" areas, others offer a choice of indoor or outdoor dining, and still others provide rooms of different sizes and decor.

The design of the kitchen, serving and dining areas is quite complex. Traffic patterns need to be carefully worked out, signs should be easy to read, work areas must be efficient. It is a job best given to a food service consultant.

Employees of AT&T Long Lines Eastern Region, Oakton (VA), relax in a two-story cafeteria replete with indoor plants, informal oak furniture, and views on two levels of seating. The designers were Kohn, Pedersen, Fox and dePolo/Dunbar. (Photograph by © Ezra Stoller/Esto)

A lively feeling is imparted to the employee lounge at Liddel, Sapp, Zivley, Brown & LaBoon, attorneys, Houston, by ISD's use of checkerboard flooring and bright colors. (Photograph by Mark Ross)

As designed by Llewelyn Davies Associates, Davis Brody Associates and Kenneth Parker Associates the cafeteria at Arco Chemical and Engineering Center, Philadelphia, is a celebration of folk art in Pennsylvania. (Photograph by Tom Crane)

There is a chance of spotting wildlife from a next door forest preserve from the cafeteria designed by Holabird & Root for Hollister, a health care products concern in Libertyville (IL). (Photograph by Howard Kaplan)

Framed prints by Richard Lindner and futuristic plastic furniture make a distinctive lunch room for Charfoos & Charfoos, attorneys, in Detroit. The designer was Jeanne Hartnett & Associates. (Photograph by Yuichi Idaka)

A cafeteria designed by Peter A. Lendrum/Interior Architecture for Southwest Forest Industries, Phoenix. (Photograph by Al Payne © 1981)

BELOW
Employee dining designed by Deupi and Associates for Rozansky & Kay Construction, Bethesda (MD). (Photograph by Ron Solomon/ Eileen Brown © 1982)

OPPOSITE
The lunch room of BEA Assoc., investment advisers, was designed by Tod Williams. (Photograph by Mark Ross)

The Meredith Corporation cafeteria adjoins a second-floor terrace in Des Moines, IO, designed by Charles Herbert and Associates. (Photograph by Architectural Fotographics/Paul S. Kivett)

Abundant trees and a soaring ceiling in reflective metal tile give the Stamford (CT) cafeteria of Champion International the outdoor ambience intended by its designer, Ulrich Franzen & Associates. (Photograph by Nick Wheeler)

MIDDLE MANAGEMENT

Middle management is very much caught in the "middle" between the executives they report to and the employees they supervise. Because they must somehow find the solitude to make management decisions while involved up-to-their-elbows in daily operations, their work area should offer visual and acoustic privacy and encourage their accessibility. These are conflicting needs, as any pressured mid-manager will tell you.

The middle manager's office sees a lot of traffic and needs sturdy, sensible fabrics and furniture. Usually, they receive the basic desk, low-backed executive chair, credenza and visitors' chairs. If they also receive outside visitors, they might have two lounge chairs as well. Just the basics.

Traditionally, middle management had enclosed offices, but today they are frequently being asked to surrender them for an open plan. Yet the middle manager is moving ahead with the computer as he now has the information to make decisions he used to pass along.

Cool white cabinetry, warm wood surfaces and upholstery make this manager's office at USA Today, *Gannett's national newspaper in Rosslyn (VA) a welcome place to work. The design was by Environmental Planning and Research. (Photograph by © Peter Aaron/Esto)*

In the manager's office at Weyerhaeuser Co., Tacoma, designed by Skidmore, Owings & Merrill, San Francisco, are a work station, conference area and 24-ft. high view of the forest. (Photograph by Jaime Ardiles-Arce)

OPPOSITE TOP
New York's Judson Realty, by Christopher H. L. Owen, gives managers glass-fronted offices with sliding doors. (Photograph by Norman McGrath)

A chair rail, fabric wallcovering, and wood furniture are used by Hellmuth, Obata & Kassabaum to create traditional looking trust offices for Flagship Bank, Miami. (Photograph by Tom Crane)

A mock up of a manager's office for ARCO Oil & Gas, Dallas, tests futuristic concepts proposed by Neville Lewis Associates. (Photograph courtesy Neville Lewis Associates)

OPPOSITE
Custom oak cabinetry designed by Deupi and Associates for Rozansky & Kay Construction, Bethesda (MD), gives distinction to an in-house architect's office. (Photograph by Ron Solomon/ Eileen Brown © 1982)

RIGHT
Equality at Diamond Shamrock Industrial Chemicals, Dallas, designed by Harwood K. Smith & Partners, includes cherry veneer furniture and an atrium view (Photograph by © Greg Hursley)

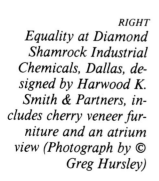

GENERAL OFFICES

Most corporations today are using open plan systems in their general office areas. But before going to any new plan, a company should consider how much visual and acoustic privacy is desirable for each employee. If needs vary, then perhaps the work situations should vary as well.

The problem is how to give each individual a sense of his own dignity and uniqueness when everyone is being treated as equals. One solution is to offer choice whenever possible and to allow employees to personalize their work stations. The results may not be to the designer's liking, but people need to feel they have control over their own workplace before they can truly identify with the company.

To be a productive worker, each employee must have a work area large enough to accommodate the paperwork, equipment and other paraphernalia needed to do the job. The work station should adjust to individual work styles and varying dimensions. The space should not seem crowded. Lighting should be adequate and adjustable, if possible. And, finally, the color and design should positively support the work effort.

A sweeping view of the Bay is shared by members of the general staff at the offices of Banque Paribas' Miami agency, designed by Richard Plumer Interior Design. Sleek work stations, light fixtures and accessories complement the modern lines of the building. (Photograph by Dan Forer)

Brightly painted tubular caps identify departments at Van de Kamp's, food processors, Long Beach. The designer was Swimmer, Cole, Martinez, Curtis. (Photograph by Sheldon Lettich)

Mid-Atlantic Toyota's staff occupies an office in Glen Burnie (MD) designed by Frank O. Gehry as a village of sharply angular walls. (Photograph by Ron Solomon)

Gensler and Associates devised playful walls and exposed ceilings to move Young & Rubicam, San Francisco, into a 19th-century brick warehouse. (Photograph by Jaime Ardiles-Arce)

ARCO Metals general offices in Rolling Meadows (IL) by Lee Manners and Associates follow ARCO standards in using open plan work stations with fabric panels and task/ambient light. (Photograph by © Peter Aaron/Esto)

To adapt quickly to any changes, the Doody Co., store planners based in Columbus (OH), asked the Design Collective to create offices that could be easily reconfigured. (Photograph by Hedrich-Blessing)

Jack L. Gordon, Architects, made New York operations for A.G. Becker more attractive by exposing the air ducts and light fixtures. (Photograph by Jan Staller)

Files and work stations, neatly tailored in wood and plastic laminate, orient personnel to the corridors of Reliance Group Holdings in New York, designed by Gwathmey Siegel & Associates. (Photograph by Jaime Ardiles-Arce)

Sweeping horizontal lines in the architecture and furnishings of general offices designed by Peter A. Lendrum Associates/Interior Architecture and Metz, Train & Youngren for Southwest Forest Industries, Phoenix, create a strong sense of place. (Photograph by Al Payne © 1981)

Virtually everyone at Best Products, catalog showroom merchandisers, Richmond (VA), has a semi-private work station designed by Hardy, Holzman, Pfeiffer. (Photograph by Norman McGrath)

RECREATION

Corporations are realizing that all work and no play does indeed make Jack and Jill not only dull, but less productive workers as well. To encourage optimum physical and psychological health, many companies are providing recreation on the premises in the form of lounges, libraries, classes of all description, exercise rooms, jogging tracks, squash and tennis courts. . . . The list could go on and on, as the realities and possibilities are as varied as employees' interests.

The best way to find out what recreation your company's employees would like is to ask them. Even non-users will get the message: the company cares about them.

Generally, these should be lighthearted areas with stimulating color and fanciful design; but some libraries and lounges might stress soft hues and comfortable seating. Whatever the direction, the aim is to create a new experience—an environment quite unlike the employees' work areas.

At the executive lounge at International Paper, New York, designed by The Space Design Group, long, low furniture, warm colors and fine materials provide intimacy and comfort. (Photograph by Mark Ross)

Television, reading and billiards are activities accommodated in the Prudential lounge, Plymouth (MN), designed by Powell/Kleinschmidt and The Architectural Alliance. (Photograph by Jim Hedrich/Hedrich-Blessing)

A tapestry inspired by Amish quilts was created by Herbert Bayer as the focal point of a lounge at ARCO Chemical and Engineering Research Center, Philadelphia, designed by Llewelyn Davies Associates, Davis Brody Associates and Kenneth Parker Associates. (Photograph by Tom Crane)

Park style seating and a Japanese waterfall are beneath a hanging garden in the lounge designed by SCR Design Organization for Geer DuBois, a New York advertising agency. (Photograph by Mark Ross)

BELOW
One's gaze is immediately drawn to the fireplace in the lounge designed by Kallmann, McKinnell & Wood with Louis Beal and Joseph Rosen of ISD for the American Academy of Arts and Sciences, Cambridge (MA) because of its fine workmanship in plaster, stone and wood. (Photograph by Jaime Ardiles-Arce)

Rowing apparatus is part of Champion International's health and fitness center at headquarters in Stamford (CT) designed by Ulrich Franzen & Associates. (Photograph by Nick Wheeler)

A library curves around a reception atrium at ARCO Chemical and Engineering Research Center, Philadelphia, designed by Llewelyn Davies Associates, Davis Brody Associates and Kenneth Parker Associates. (Photograph by Tom Crane)

OPPOSITE
Small gatherings can be held at Meredith Corp., Des Moines, in a pastel colored lounge bathed in sunlight, designed by Charles Herbert & Associates. (Photograph by Architectural Fotographics/Paul S. Kivett)

CIRCULATION

Back–lit panels in staggered formation give a corridor at Gulf States Utilities Co., Beaumont (TX), a sense of weightless movement; the designer was Morris-Aubry. (Photograph by chas mcgrath)

What could be interesting about halls and stairs and escalators? Plenty. Of course, they could also be boringly straight and white with no relief. But increasingly they are being used by architects and designers in the most playful ways—undulating walls, bright colors, unexpected juxtapositions of forms, neon lighting, show-stopping art. Here, distraction is needed and appreciated; stimulation perks up the spirit.

Circulation areas are neutral spaces that separate functions. Because they are no one's territory, people commonly have serious conversations there. Perhaps corporations should scatter small, informal seating areas to encourage these important chance meetings.

Distinct circulation routes should actually make it easier to find one's way through the corporate maze, but there are two precautions: keep signage distinct and do not block the exit signs.

Hellmuth, Obata & Kassabaum's design for the escalators at MCAUTO, St. Louis, gives computer technicians a fast, exciting ride. (Photograph by Nathan Benn)

Advertising for clients lines the corridor at J. Walter Thompson, New York, designed by Griswold, Heckel & Kelly. (Photograph by Ashod Kassabian)

Columns define a circulation area in a New York renovated warehouse office designed by Stephen Levine Architects. (Photograph by Norman McGrath)

Visitors at the main entry of Reliance Group Holdings, New York, designed by Gwathmey Siegel & Associates, are immediately oriented by the interconnecting staircase. (Photograph by Jaime Ardiles-Arce)

LEFT

A grid on paneling and carpet in Meredith Corp., Des Moines, is counterpointed by curved walls in the design by Charles Herbert & Assoc. (Photograph by Assassi)

OPPOSITE

The 1926 main administration building of Warner Bros., Burbank (CA), features a luminous stairway, beautifully restored by Swimmer, Cole, Martinez, Curtis. (Photograph by Toshi Yoshimi)

At Best Products, catalog showroom merchandisers, Richmond (VA), the design by Hardy, Holzman, Pfeiffer creates very memorable crossroads. (Photograph by Norman McGrath)

ART COLLECTION

Modern architecture and interior design often present office workers with too stark an environment to sustain long hours of sedentary white collar work. Art programs help to make the office environment more enjoyable for its occupants.

Of course, being associated with art also confers social status and prestige on the owner or donor, a respectability that corporations are pleased to have. It can even be argued that art collecting, as part of an effort to support the arts, has helped many a business in softening the charges of its social critics. The Revenue Act of 1935, which declared that five percent of corporate income is deductible as a charitable contribution, gives corporate support of the arts its legal underpinning as a tax reduction strategy. And, finally, good art tends to appreciate handsomely.

The advantages of corporate art collecting are so numerous and varied, they cannot be measured in traditional business terms.

On the executive floor of USA Today, *Gannett's national newspaper in Rosslyn (VA), a six-month rotating art exhibit arrangement with the Renwick Gallery in Washington brings new works by young American artists to be seen against the stark design by Environmental Planning and Research. (Photograph by © Peter Aaron/Esto)*

A 50-foot mural by Kim Plavcan brightens the dining room of Dual-Lite headquarters in Newtown (CT), designed by Eve Frankl, ASID. (Photograph by Norman McGrath)

OPPOSITE
Among the many works of art at Best Products, catalog showroom merchandisers, Richmond (VA) are those by Andy Warhol, Neil Welliver and Jack Beal; the headquarters were designed by Hardy, Holzman, Pfeiffer. (Photograph by Norman McGrath)

"Childhood of Hephaestus," a painting by Ian Tornak, gives an ethereal feeling to a reception area at Xerox headquarters, Stamford (CT), designed by ISD. (Photograph by Jaime Ardiles-Arce)

ABOVE
Adolph Gottlieb's 1961 oil is part of the renowned art program at Chase Manhattan Bank in New York City.

ABOVE

Photography is actively collected for the offices of Kimberly-Clark in Neenah (WI), designed by Hellmuth, Obata & Kassabaum. The images, which depict aspects of the international markets where the company is active, feature the work of four well-known photographers, Burt Glinn, Ernst Haas, Art Kane and Jay Maisel. There are 258 images in all.

OPPOSITE

The main executive corridor of International Paper headquarters in New York, designed by The Space Design Group, is handled as an art gallery. Visible here are a Japanese mulberry paper collage by Maud Morgan and egg-shaped and pedestal sculptures by Pino Pedano. (Photograph by Mark Ross)

IV   Corporate Furnishings

*"Office images are created to influence behavior,
to win clients
—to gain power."*
FRANKLIN BECKER

Some offices are distinguished by unusual architecture, others by a spectacular view, but most are distinguished (if distinguished at all) by their furnishings. Furnishings are such things as desks, seating, tables, storage units, fabrics, art and accessories, and even the machines that make the modern office functional and competitive. For our purposes, the finishing elements that become part and parcel of the architecture can also be considered furnishings—cabinetry and woodworking, flooring, as well as wall, ceiling, lighting and window treatments.

Furnishings can be looked at in two ways: how their *form* supports an employee's work effort and how they reinforce his *image*. Office furnishings are potent work tools that either help or hinder the employee. Whether the employee is aware of it or not, the work environment is molding his behavior and the opinion of others. A passive environment does not exist.

FORM: THE PHYSICAL COMPONENTS OF FURNISHINGS

Every office worker is the same in that he needs a work surface, storage facilities and a seat. After that, every worker is different because human dimension and body size vary widely and because each person develops his own unique style of working. It is difficult to conceive of a basic office that would be right for everyone. Yet, since an office is much like a stage set with its ever-changing cast of characters, most corporations do not allow a great degree of individual choice for furnishings—unless the office belongs to an officer or key employee.

WORK SURFACE

The work surface, or desk, is the most important element in the office. When we consider how much time a worker spends at his desk (it is estimated to be more than half of his waking hours), it is a wonder the desk has not been given more attention. Kleeman (*The Challenge of Interior Design*), says that ergonomic research done by the Aerospace Medical Research Laboratories of the U.S. Air Force, as well as by Sweden, Germany, Holland, and particularly Great Britain, has produced an abundance of data that could be used to design more functional desks.[1]

"Currently the typical American desk is made for just two types of people: the tall and the very tall," states Kleeman. A severe problem, he feels, as "Ergonomic studies show not only a definite connection between bad working-surface heights and lower back pain but also a connection between these heights and

In the reception area of Alusuisse of America, a Swiss holding company in New York City, architect/designer Samuel De Santo has used the black granite of the floor to create a reception desk. A pair of chrome and glass adjustable tables, designed by Eileen Gray in the 1930s, stand in front of a sofa to the right (not seen in this photograph). To make the area work as a whole, De Santo has repeated the grid design of the floor in a wood-framed, mirrored wall and vaulted ceiling. The result is a contemporary space with an image of great strength and class. (Photograph by Mark Ross)

wrist-forearm problems, too."[2] Although ergonomists suggest that the work surface be adjustable—with a height range of 26½ to 31 inches for desks and 20½ to 26½ inches for typing surfaces—most desks are 29 to 30 inches high and most typing surfaces 26 or 27 inches high.[3] American manufacturers are beginning to produce adjustable work surfaces, particularly for use with the new electronic office equipment, but the range and ease of adjustment of the American products still falls short of Swedish and Japanese models. (Standards for office chair durability and safety are promulgated in the United States by the Business and Institutional Furniture Manufacturers Association and the American National Standards Institute; however, there are no U.S. industry or government standards for ergonomic office chair design, whereas government standards in Germany, Sweden, and Japan are quite explicit.)

The shape and size of the working surface should be matched to the worker's reach and needs. Usually only the area within seated reach is used for work tasks, while the remainder of the surface (the ends and edges) tends to be used for storage and memorabilia. (Einstein was a user of these outlying areas, as his work style required piles of papers kept close at hand; he reputedly termed it "meaningful clutter."[4])

For workers who want the maximum amount of work surface within reach, a half-donut shape is suggested, with a modified L-shape next in efficiency. The rectangular shape is least efficient, but the most popular. The half-donut shape might be a good choice for an individual office, but would require more floor space than the rectangle or modified L-shape if used in a general office area. Also, its curved edges would not fit the grid layout of most offices.

The first constructed work surfaces were probably tables. Today, many executives are returning to a table/desk, finding that it is more conducive for informal meetings than the traditional desk. However, if an executive opts for an enclosed desk, an overhang on the visitor's side should be considered. An overhang allows visitors to get closer to the desk, and, therefore, to the executive; a flat-front

An adjustable Swedish desk puts the work surface on telescoping legs and keeps the storage units separate for flexibility. (Photograph courtesy of Facit AB)

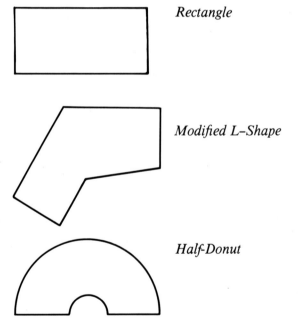

Rectangle

Modified L-Shape

Half-Donut

Worksurface shape and size should be matched to the worker's reach and needs. Although the rectangle is most popular, it offers the least amount of reachable space; while the half-donut shape offers the greatest amount. The modified L-shape is between the rectangle and half-donut in efficiency, but fits a grid better than the half-donut.

desk insures that the participants will remain at a set distance. The choice should be determined by how the desk area is to be used and how the executive wishes it to influence the behavior of his visitors.

Some executives like the table/desk because it has connotations of power—since it has no attached storage, it suggests the user is a people motivater rather than a paper pusher. The executive makes the decisions, his subordinates implement them. Of course, even the most powerful executive does touch hand to paper, but it is a good fantasy that the clean table/desk helps support. One furniture company executive goes so far as to keep *all* papers out of sight—well hidden in the credenza behind his table/desk.

INFORMATION STORAGE

Information, in its many forms, is the quiddity of the office. The problems come in deciding what information is to be stored, in what form, and where. Since the time of Louis XIV, when cabinetmakers got the idea of incorporating the chest of drawers with the table (thus giving birth to the modern desk)[5], people have been using personal desk drawers for all manner of inefficient storage—from filing papers that should be generally available to stashing old shoes and galoshes. It is the desk drawers, in fact, that prevent desks from becoming truly adjustable. So why do most desks have drawers?

Many researchers and designers feel other storage systems would be more usable. Leslie Capek, an architect, thinks that "Everything should be stored in jars, racks, trays, bins, bowls or whatever to keep it visible and accessible while discouraging private stashes and squirrelling [sic] of community property."[6] Environmental psychologist Robert Sommer has suggested that storage should not be out of sight, but should serve as "visual triggers" to remind the worker of undone tasks.[7] For this reason, some manufacturers have put files in the top of the desk, covered with a tambour or a flip top; others have created rolling, open file bins; and most open plan systems have incorporated a push-pin panel above the work surface.

Although there is talk of it, file cabinets have not yet been completely replaced by the floppy disk or other means of electronic storage. In fact, when most corporations today move into a new space, they end up not only renovating the old filing cabinets by electrostatic painting, but buying additional new ones as well. Because the hard surface of file cabinets interferes with acoustical privacy in open plan offices, many companies have attempted to centralize the files away from the work areas. But this is not always convenient.

Basically, there are two types of file cabinets: *vertical* files in which the drawer is filled from front to back; and *lateral* files in which the files fill the drawers from side to side. The lateral files were more recently developed, protrude less into the circulation area than vertical files, and are generally favored by architects and designers for their contemporary look. Both types come in two-, three-, and four-drawer sizes; and while most office construction can support a height of six drawers, it is difficult to use files stacked higher than four drawers.

For long-term or archival storage, mobile file units which move along special floor tracks, are useful; but because these concentrated stacks result in extreme floor loading, they cannot be used in some locations.

OFFICE MACHINES

"Office automation" refers to the integrated use of computer and communications systems to support the administrative procedures of an organization. It may take the form of word processing, electronic message systems, teleconferencing, facsimile transmission, electronic filing systems, on-line calendar systems, and hook-ups to the corporation's files and other outside services. Its importance to corporations is two-fold, as it offers a hope of improving the productivity of clerical and managerial employees and it may be the only way to handle information processing in an increasingly complex and changing future.[8]

At this point, its long-range effect on the design of operations can only be guessed. What we do know now, is that the form of the

*Gwathmey Siegel & Associates designed the New York City headquarters of Reliance Group Holdings Inc. to convey an image of permanence, quality and substance. All A-level offices have a custom credenza that incorporates a closet, storage compartments and a tackboard. They also include two areas for meetings—the desk with an overhang on the visitor's side (to allow the visitor to move in closer), and a small conference table. Note that the executive's chair appears to be no more grand than the visitors' chairs.
(Photograph by Jaime Ardiles-Arce)*

At the Houston City Bank, Morris/Aubry has furnished the chairman's office in 18th-century reproductions and antiques and has given the room a gracious sense of history with architectural woodworking—the chair rail, fan light and multi-paned doors. The look is warm and residential and suggests that the bank has been in this spot for centuries, yet the building was built in the 1950s. (Photograph by Rick Gardner)

technology is changing daily and requires both organizations and facilities which are flexible and capable of responding quickly. For this reason, new buildings are being constructed with power lines accessible in all office areas, whether they are currently needed or not; and "adjustability" and "flexibility" have become the catchwords of systems furniture representatives.

SEATING

Executive and boardroom chairs are often chosen for their impressive size, rather than for their comfort. For an executive who is rarely at his desk or a board member who may not sit for more than a couple hours at a meeting, such a chair might suffice. But for those employees who spend most work hours at their desk, seating discomfort can affect both productivity and health.

Because the "average" person does not exist, it is crucial that personal office chairs have an adjustable seat height and backrest. Most office chairs do adjust, but their lowest position is often not low enough for a short person. Ergonomists Kroemer and Robinette suggest that the seat height should have an adjustability range from $13\frac{2}{3}$ inches to $20\frac{2}{3}$ inches, so the worker can place both feet on the floor when his thighs are in a horizontal position.[9] (Their specifications are based on 29 separate studies in five countries, which correspond with NASA's worldwide anthropometric data as well.)

If the feet are not touching the floor, the back of the thighs receive pressure and circulation is partially cut off below the knees; bloodclots, varicose veins and enlarged calves can be the result. According to Kleeman, the worker in a too-high chair will usually sit on the front edge, at first in an upright posture, but then ". . . the back and abdominal muscles become fatigued, and the result is a slumped position which makes it quite difficult to pay attention to what is going on, or even work at all."[10] To help relieve pressure on the thighs, most manufacturers curve the front edge of the seat downwards; a few also offer seats with a front tilt adjustment.

When the spine is slumped over forward,

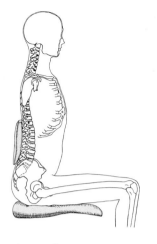

Personal seating should encourage an upright sitting posture by supporting the lower back and allowing both feet to be on the floor when the thighs are in a horizontal position. For truly dynamic and healthful seating, the chair back should move with the worker as he leans forward and back, and it is vital that both the back and seat heights be adjustable. (Illustration courtesy of Domore)

there is pressure on the intervertebral disks and the discs lose tissue fluid. To encourage an upright seating position, most office chairs provide a built-in cushion support for the lower back area. This support should adjust up or down to suit the user. It is also desirable for the chair to have an adjustable tension spring back that can move slightly forward, as well as back, to give the user a variety of correct seating positions—moving forward to back keeps the discs supplied with fluid and helps prevent back problems.

Armrests can aid the shifting of weight and can relieve the spinal column of some stress; however, they can also hinder movement if they are permanently attached to a fixed chair back, or prevent the user from getting close to the work surface. Some manufacturers provide removable arms.

Besides providing comfortable seating, the chair should be safe. To prevent toppling, the chair should span a circle equal to, or greater than, the seat width in diameter. European chairs are required to have five-prong bases for better stability. American chairs are generally converting from four-prong to five-prong bases.

Once the chair is adjusted to the user, ergonomists suggest that the working surface height correspond to the height of the seating surface—a desk surface should be 10 to 12 inches higher, a typing surface 5½ to 7 inches (or higher if more thigh room is needed). Yet, since most work surfaces are not adjustable, employees will just have to "make do."

As early as the first quarter of the century, office management studies suggested that the desk and chair work together as an integrated whole. Even then, designers saw the need for footrests, for workers to have the option of standing or sitting to work, and for writing surfaces that were tilted at an angle. Today, it is still a rare office that incorporates these revolutionary design ideas.

IMAGE: THE CULTURAL EXPRESSION OF FORM AND WHAT IT MEANS

After an employee has an idea of what he needs in his office or work area to do an effective job, the next question is how that employee wishes to be seen by his fellow workers and by visitors. Employees within an organization know to what extent personal expression is allowed within their company and will judge fellow employees with that in mind; everyone is, nevertheless, judged by the appearance of his office as much as by personal dress and grooming.

If your office looks like everyone else's, you are likely to be thought of as just another cog in the wheel. If it looks too unusual, others might think you do not fit in. The image of your office can let visitors know just how conservative or unconventional you are, what your interests are outside the office, if you have a family, how organized you are, how intellectual, how artistic, and how highly you think of yourself.

The clues are to be found in obvious places such as photos of your favorite boat, horse, child or politician; the titles of the books on your shelf; the art on your wall; your awards and trophies; and the signs of your hobbies—everything from prized collections to golf ball paperweights!

The clues are also hidden in the office's subtle indicators of quality—the materials of which the furnishings are made and the style of the furnishings themselves.

• Natural materials such as wood, stone, and leather suggest substance, endurance and tradition; while synthetics usually suggest their opposites (unless the synthetic could be mistaken for the natural—for example, nylon upholstery fabric that looks and feels like wool—but wood-grained plastic laminate and other obvious fakeries are to be avoided).

• The hardness or softness of the materials lets visitors know whether this is a formal, strictly business office (hard seats) or a more informal "let's get comfortable" type of place (soft cushions).

• A shiny, reflective finish (on a table or desk, for example) is more formal than a dull or matte finish. Glass, mirror, polished stone and high-gloss wood finishes are therefore more formal than leather, slate or natural finished wood.

• Warm colors (those with red and yellow tones) encourage people to interact, while cool colors (those with blue and green tones) set a psychological distance. Cool colors encourage introspection and are thus good for open plan work areas where quiet, solitary work is desired.

• Construction features such as hand-crafted, as opposed to machine produced, and custom-detailed, rather than standard, are signs of quality furnishings. The cabinet with 21 coats of lacquer, French dovetailed joints and hand-polished hardware is to be found only in the offices of a select few—its exclusivity reflects the high standards and status of its owner.

Materials can make a significant difference in establishing image. For example, a large construction company in the Northeast has a father and son as president and executive vice president, respectively. The father's personality is all business without a glimmer of warmth. His son, "Mr. Nice Guy," has difficulty seeing himself as a power figure. When the company's headquarters were redesigned, the interior architect let the father and son's offices compensate for their shortcomings.

The father was given a predominately red office with warm-toned paintings, textured fabrics, and soft, well-cushioned seating—everything to make the visitor feel welcome and comfortable, and encourage interaction. While the son's office was done in blue, with a stainless steel table/deck and modern, hard-seated visitor's chairs. His art consisted of a collection of glass obelisks on glass shelves. The effect was cool and authoritative. Both offices, in their extremes, helped to reinforce new executive images.

FURNITURE STYLES

The style of furniture is often used to suggest a desired personal or corporate image. Yet the history of furniture is as complicated as history itself, and many people forego getting involved altogether once they have had a few encounters with "early this" and "late that." It is not necessary to be an expert on furniture to furnish one's office in antiques or classic designs, as interior designers are in the business of helping others determine what style will work best for them; but it is helpful to have some knowledge of what is old and new, as well as the image different styles of furniture project.

Furniture can be separated into three categories: period styles and period reproductions; transitional; and modern.

Period and period reproductions are true antiques and new pieces that are faithful copies of antiques. An antique that is of a useful design and structurally sound can distinguish an office; yet sometimes such pieces are impossible to find at affordable prices. Fine reproductions can then give the pleasure of an original (although connoisseurs can usually tell the difference) and 20th-century glues and other new methods of construction will insure stability. Because fine reproductions are made by an ever diminishing number of craftsmen and basically still by hand, these pieces, while less expensive than antiques, are still substantial investments.

The following furniture styles are frequently used in corporate settings:
• The French styles of the kings **Louis XIV, XV** and **XVI** are ornately carved and often

gilded. Their ostentatious look of luxury is not for most offices, but their feminine and formal image is right for certain style-related businesses.

• **Queen Anne, Chippendale, Chinese Chippendale, Sheraton, Adam** and **Hepplewhite** had their origins in 18th-century England. These were the styles that were imported by the wealthy colonial families and they have since been the favorite styles of prestigious law firms, insurance companies and accountants—professions that are enhanced by an image of stability and tradition. Also used in the "leather sofa and oriental carpet-type" men's clubs, these styles confer class by association. Most pieces are of mahogany, a few of walnut. Leather in colors, and luxurious fabrics such as brocades, damasks, velvets, and mohair have traditionally been used to upholster these styles.

• **American Colonial** style refers to the more simple and modest versions of the 18th-century furniture mentioned above that were made by American cabinetmakers during the 18th and 19th centuries. The image is warm and comforting.

• In the 19th century, **English Regency, French Directoire,** and **Empire** were originally influenced by the neo-classic decorations of palaces. Used in government and other older office buildings, these styles bespeak authority, dignity and power.

• **Gothic** furniture styles derived from the 19th-century Gothic Revival in England are associated with universities and religious institutions. The image is one of solidity, conservatism and enduring values.

An 18th-century French armchair. (Photograph from The Metropolitan Museum of Art, Gift of J. Pierpont Morgan, 1906)

A Queen Anne armchair made between 1725-1750. (Photograph from The Metropolitan Museum of Art, Rogers Fund, 1925)

An 18th-century Queen Anne wing chair from New England. (Photograph from The Metropolitan Museum of Art, Gift of Mrs. J. Insley Blair, 1950)

An 18th-century mahogany Chippendale side chair is distinguished by claw-and-ball feet. (Photograph from The Metropolitan Museum of Art, Bequest of Cecile L. Mayer, 1962)

A carved, walnut armchair in the style of Hepplewhite, was made in Philadelphia between 1790-1810. (Photograph courtesy of Christie's)

A Chinese Chippendale fret back armchair reproduced from the original. (Photograph courtesy of Smith & Watson)

A rare reproduction of an 18th-century Adam armchair made by Thomas Chippendale. (Photograph courtesy of Smith & Watson)

A bow-back Windsor armchair, made in America in the 18th century. (Photograph from The Metropolitan Museum of Art, Gift of Mrs. Russell Sage, 1909)

A Sheraton armchair reproduced from an 18th-century original in shaded mahogany. (Photograph courtesy of Smith & Watson)

An early 19th-century Regency armchair. (Photograph courtesy of Christie's)

A reproduction of an 18th-century Sheraton bamboo armchair. (Photograph courtesy of Smith & Watson)

A rare Empire white-painted and gilt armchair, made in Baltimore between 1825–35. (Photograph courtesy of Christie's)

- **Victorian** oak furniture of the late 19th century can give a 20th-century office charm. The image is one of substance, with a down-to-earth home-like quality. Here only the originals will do, as they have a massive, heavy look that the reproductions lack.

- **Mission Oak** is a severely plain and rectilinear style of furniture made in America between 1900 and 1916. Fostered by the international Arts and Crafts Movement, mission oak was part of the attempt to raise everyday objects to the level of fine art through hand-craftsmanship and good design. Although it was to be timeless in its appeal, mission oak was forgotten until the 1970s. Its growing popularity is evident in its price; pieces which sold for hundreds of dollars in the 1970s sell for thousands today. Its image is strong and unpretentious.

- **Mexican colonial** and **Spanish** styles are growing in popularity in the Southwest. Another sturdy look, it is strong on warmth if the setting is of the same period. If done inexpensively or half-way, there is the danger of a theatrical image.

Transitional furniture includes the many styles that are not faithful reproductions and not modern. Transitional falls in the middle and in its indecisiveness has a "neither here nor there" quality. It is what furniture manufacturers call a "look." A group of desks may have an "Early American" look suggested by a few Early American design details. Transitional styles are watered-down versions of reproductions for buyers who do not want to make a strong statement or who cannot tell the difference. The quality varies, but the price is much less than faithful reproductions.

Modern design is usually thought of as clean in line and honest in feeling. But because modern has existed for a number of years, it can be differentiated into subcategories such as Bauhaus, Art Deco, Fifties-Modern, High-Tech and the contemporary modern furniture being designed today.

The Victorian office is typified by the oak furnishings in the office of Success Magazine *at the turn of the century. (Photograph from the Museum of the City of New York)*

A Frank Lloyd Wright armchair, probably designed in 1902–3, was typical of Mission Oak furniture. (Photograph from The Metropolitan Museum of Art, Purchase, Emily C. Chadbourne Bequest, 1972)

Although this chair was made in New England in the early 18th century, its front legs and stretcher were inspired by Spanish furniture. (Photograph from The Metropolitan Museum of Art, Gift of Mrs. Russell Sage, 1909)

The Wassily chair was the first bent tubular-steel chair designed by Marcel Breuer at the Bauhaus in 1925. (Photograph courtesy of Knoll International)

An Art Deco side chair from France. (Photograph from The Metropolitan Museum of Art, Purchase, Edward C. Moore, Jr. Gift, 1925)

An example of Fifties-Modern *is the office furniture components designed by Maria Bergson. (Photographs courtesy of Maria Bergson)*

- **Bauhaus** originated in Germany's famed school of design in the 1920s, and this so-called International Style was stripped of non-essential elements to achieve a mating of art and technology. The materials used are chiefly leather, chrome tubing, bent wood, caning and glass. Its image is professional and strong, if somewhat cool. It implies good taste, elegance and money.

- **Art Deco** is the look of the 1920s and 1930s ocean liners—streamlined, rounded corners, zig-zag motifs, glass-like lacquered surfaces, lots of black, white, grey, rose and pale green. The image is one of glamour, but not substance.

- **Fifties-Modern** consists of blond oak furniture, plastic laminate surfaces, boomerang-shaped legs on tables and chairs—furniture many of us remember as new. Today it is already being collected by connoisseurs of fine furniture.

- **High-Tech** was born in the late 1960s, a play on the words high-style and technology, and is the use of utilitarian industrial equipment and materials as furnishings, or as an inspiration for sleek, highly refined designs that look technological, whether or not they actually are. The image can be futuristic and imply progress. A natural fit with electronic office equipment; at its best, it is fresh and colorful, at its worst, cold and inhuman. The style is epitomized by the work of Italian designers working out of Bologna and Milan.

- **Contemporary** furniture are new styles being designed today; they are often influenced by earlier modern styles. When the designs are clean and strong, the image they project will be sincerity, strength and a forward-looking approach to business.

Antique furniture can look spectacular in a modern setting, just as certain modern pieces can be a nice counterpoint to a traditional setting. Sometimes mixing the two is the answer, as the image ties a concern for values of the past with a progressive vision of the future.

DESKS

One's desk is the single most obvious embodiment of one's being in the office. For some it is a dais that magnifies importance, enlarging one's personal presence. For others it is a place of order from which the world is controlled—a noiseless black box from which power flows. But for most of us, it is a workbench—the place where our ideas are crafted and refined—and where piles of papers mix with personal treasures. A desk can conceal one's nervous knee or shoeless foot, can keep one a safe distance from others, and can showcase messy and compulsive workstyles.

The clue to an employee's importance lies in the size, shape and material of his desk. The bigger the desk, the greater his position. Important people's desks are usually large, rectangular in shape, hard and shiny. A stone desk top is status; so is glass and highly polished wood. A leather top may not be shiny, but it is tradition and tradition is status.

Table/desks are more relaxed—everyone is more exposed. If round, it de-emphasizes hierarchical structure further yet. People can get closer at a table/desk—the safe distance is diminished.

The *Wall Street Journal* reports that several chairmen of the board and presidents of major corporations are forgoing traditional desks—preferring to stand at high desks. Could this be a trend? Or does the truly active CEO need more than one workbench to test his ideas?

A monumental Georgian burl walnut pedestal desk takes the commanding position in this executive office. (Photograph courtesy of Smith & Watson)

OPPOSITE
*To maintain the light-
ness of the modern fur-
nishings within a re-
stored traditional office
for the Edward J. Safdie
Group, New York, de-
signer Charles Swerz and
Associates called for the
large desk to be made of
a marble base and a
glass top. (Photograph by
Mark Ross)*

ABOVE
*The president of Alusuisse, a Swiss holding company that deals in aluminum and other commodities, sits at a
table with a round black granite top, surrounded by seating in matching black upholstery in the New York
office designed by Samuel De Santo and Associates. (Photograph by Mark Ross)*

1 *FX Desk By Brueton*
2 *Meteora Leather Desk by Pace Collection*
3 *Bruce Hannah Desk by Knoll International*
4 *Taftville Desk by Helikon*
5 *Ken Walker Desk by ICF*
6 *7200 Executive Desk by Pace Collection*

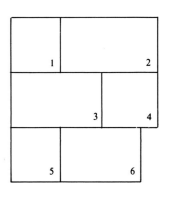

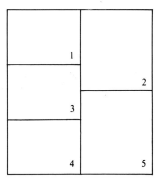

1 *LC Executive Desk by Castelli*
2 *Capsule Desk by Brickel Associates*
3 *50/7236/COOD Desk by Edward Axel Roffman*
4 *Electra Desk by Stow/Davis*
5 *Le Corbusier/6 Desk by Atelier International*

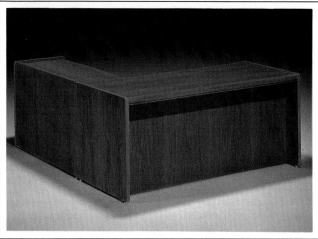

1 *Gwathmey-Siegel Desk by Knoll International*
2 *Figured Pedestal Desk by Wood & Hogan*
3 *Mahogany Desk by Conwed*
4 *Federal Style Desk with stationery boxes by Kittinger*
5 *Counting House Partner's Desk by Wood & Hogan*

1	2
3	4
	5

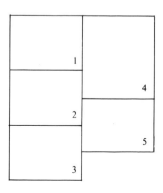

1 *George I Desk by Baker, Knapp & Tubbs*
2 *Chippendale Executive Desk by Smith & Watson*
3 *Georgian Campaign Desk by Kittinger*
4 *Georgian Campaign Table Desk by Kittinger*
5 *Chippendale Oval Desk by Baker, Knapp & Tubbs*

SEATING

In Roman times, the person who was allowed to sit in a chair was important—everyone else stood or sat on the ground. The chair was and is still the throne. When a host rises from his chair, it is time for the visitor to depart.

As in many other pieces of furniture, the size of a chair denotes its importance. Many corporations buy a range of personal chairs, then assign them according to rank, not measurements or job tasks. Executives sit in large, heavily padded chairs because their job is obstensibly to sit and make decisions. Handsome as these chairs might be, they often offer little support for the lower back and minimal adjustability. Secretaries, by contrast, are given the most dynamic and responsive seating—the best for our posture. Yet they would probably prefer a chair that denoted greater status. Middle management's chair is in between in size and is a good compromise as it offers status, support and mobility.

Chairs for operators of CRT screens and terminals present a special dilemma as the angle of the keyboard and glare on the screen determines one's posture.

Guests seated in visitors' chairs are not able or expected to move. They are on your turf and your terms. You tilt and swivel, they shift and acquiesce. Lounge seating is also stationary, but here the visitor is the true guest.

Seating in different sizes, shapes and textures are employed by Jeanne Hartnett & Associates to create a well balanced study in contrasts for the reception area of Charfoos & Charfoos, attorneys, in Detroit. (Photograph by Yuichi Idaka)

PERSONAL SEATING

1 *Diffrient Manager's Chair by Knoll International*
2 *Cyborg Chair by Rudd International*
3 *Pollack Chair by Knoll International*
4 *Moving Chair by Stow/Davis*
5 *Helena Chair by Sunar*
6 *Logos Highback Chair by Brayton International*
7 *System 15 Executive Seating by Comforto*
8 *Attache Series Seating by ii1*

		2	3
	1	4	5
6	7		8

1 *Biochair by American Seating*
2 *Babar Chair by Atelier International*
3 *MGT Management Chair by Thonet*
4 *Fabricius #5 Chair by Brayton International*
5 *Wilkhahn FS Executive Chair by Vecta Contract*
6 *Vertebra Executive Chair by Krueger*
7 *806 Executive Chair by Hardwood House*
8 *Diffrient Executive Chair by Knoll International*

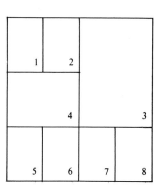

1 *Concentrx Operator's Chair by Steelcase*
2 *Director's Swivel Chair by Smith & Watson*
3 *Mobius Cane Chair by Brickel Associates*
4 *Quorum Chair by Helikon*
5 *Condenso Executive Chair by Davis*
6 *Penta 200 Chair by All-Steel*
7 *UniGroup Chair by Haworth*
8 *High Back Word Processor Chair by Madison*
9 *Executive Task Chair by Skandia*

1	2	3	4
5	6		
7	8		9

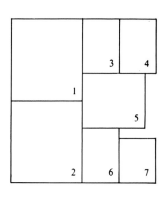

1 *Ergon Chairs by Herman Miller*
2 *Office Chairs by Schaefer Brothers*
3 *Paradigm Series Chair by Stow/Davis*
4 *Bert England Chair by Dunbar*
5 *Multiple Use Chair by Skandia*
6 *Arm Chair by Brickel Associates*
7 *Hepplewhite Barrel Swivel Chair by Smith & Watson*

  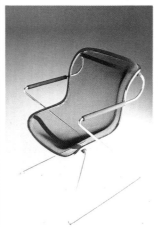 

VISITOR SEATING

1 *Grid Chair by Brickel Associates*
2 *Le Corbusier/7 Armchair by Atelier International*
3 *Penelope Chair by Castelli*
4 *rio™ Chair by Fixtures Furniture*
5 *Prague Chair by Stendig*
6 *University Chair by Brickel Associates*
7 *Wegner Armchair by Knoll International*
8 *Meteora Chair by Pace Collection*

1	2	3	4
5	6		7
	8		

1 *Chippendale Captain's Chair by Hickory Chair*
2 *Queen Anne Highback Armchair by Kittinger*
3 *Hepplewhite Barrel Chair by Smith & Watson*
4 *Chinese Chippendale Armchair by Smith & Watson*
5 *Chippendale Corner Chair by Hickory Chair*
6 *DC-1253 Chair by Dependable*
7 *Brno Chair by Thonet*
8 *Eames Molded Plywood Chair by Herman Miller*
9 *801 Arm Chair by Hardwood House*

1	2		
3	4		5
6	7	8	9

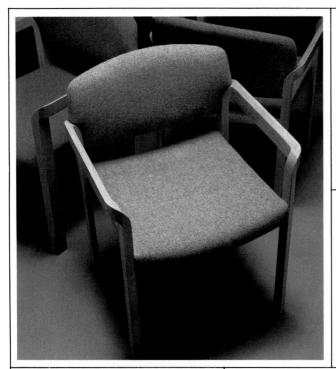

1 *Continuum Series Chair by Stow/Davis*
2 *Petitt Ply Chair by Thonet*
3 *Freyer Chair by ii1*
4 *Acorn Chairs by Sunar*
5 *Breuer Cesca Chair by Thonet*
6 *BBC156 Chair by Helikon*

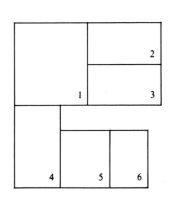

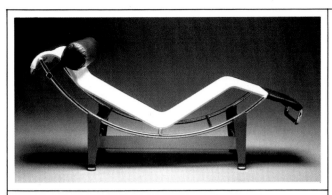

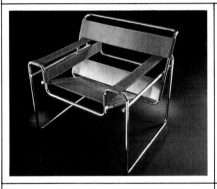

LOUNGE SEATING

1. *Le Corbusier/4 Chaise by Atelier International*
2. *Haus Koller Armchair by ICF*
3. *Fafalla Seating by ii1*
4. *Wassily Chair by Knoll International*
5. *Saladin Sofa by Stendig*
6. *Adagio Sofa by Dunbar*
7. *7070 Chair by Dunbar*
8. *Barcelona Lounge Chair by Knoll International*

1 *Stephens Lounge Chair by Knoll International*
2 *Le Corbusier/2 Armchair by Atelier International*
3 *Eames Lounge Chair and Ottoman by Herman Miller*
4 *Saarinen Collection by Knoll International*
5 *George I Chair by Smith & Watson*
6 *James River Wing Chair by Hickory Chair*
7 *Chippendale curved back sofa with rolled arm by Kittinger*
8 *Chesterfield Sofa by Smith & Watson*
9 *Delphi Settee by Helikon*

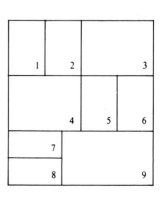

1 *Eichenberger Chair by Stendig*
2 *Nonstop Seating by Stendig*
3 *Bertoia Lounge Chair and Ottoman by Knoll International*
4 *Mississippi Seating by Castelli*
5 *Kubus Chair by ICF*
6 *Wegner Peacock Chair by Knoll International*
7 *Cartouche Chair by Brickel Associates*
8 *Platner Lounge Chair and Ottoman by Knoll International*

TABLES

Tables, like people, come in all shapes and sizes. The conference table is the grandest of them all. Some are so large they have to be sawed in half to be moved. Some are a grouping of smaller tables which can be pushed together or apart as needed. *The* status symbol for the corporation, after the building itself, the conference table is most formal and important in stone, but wood has warmth. Wood is also easily crafted into numerous shapes—the horseshoe, circular and rectangle, with the rectangle being the most hierarchical and most popular. Shaping the table slightly wider at its middle than at its ends allows everyone to see and hear.

Coffee tables are good for informal meetings. They become the focus and serve as a common ground for resting cups and papers. As a small barrier, coffee tables allow people to gather at a closer social distance. Occasional tables beside lounge seating provide places to put things down.

And then there are the utilitarian tables—the lunchroom table, the table for collating reports, the adjustable tables for computer machines. Some architects and designers feel we should use individual tables for all personal office equipment—that the typing surface commonly attached to secretarial desks forces left- and right-handed workers into the same fixed positions. Individual tables would permit choice and control over one's own work style. It is a new, old idea.

A custom table in wood with leather insert furnishes a dignified setting and complements the proportions and detailing of the small conference room of the American Academy of Arts and Sciences, Cambridge (MA), designed by Kallman, McKinnell & Wood with Louis Beal and Joseph Rosen of ISD. (Photograph by Jaime Ardiles-Arce)

A corner conference room at Diamond Shamrock headquarters, Dallas, designed by PLM Design. (Photograph by Mark Ross)

Circular and rounded table tops in wood and glass and cylindrical bases in metal and wood act as common elements throughout Arco Metals offices, Rolling Meadows (IL), designed by Lee Manners & Associates. Shown here are an informal executive conference room and an executive office. (Photograph by © Peter Aaron/Esto)

A walnut conference table in the Queen Anne style and walnut paneling to match constitute a dignified conference room for Drexel Burnham Lambert's Providence office, designed by Mayers & Schiff Associates. (Photograph by Roger Birn)

Table tops in Paradiso marble and teak with nephrite jade center inlays dominate the board room at Diamond Shamrock headquarters, Dallas, designed by PLM Design. (Photograph by Mark Ross)

1   *Radial Extension Table by Smith & Watson*
2   *Radial Extension Table by Smith & Watson*
3   *T1311 Table-Desk by Helikon*
4   *Dalman Marble Table by Casa Nova*
5   *ASI Oval Marble Top Conference Table by Intrex*
6   *ASI Marble Top Cube Base Table by Intrex*

1	2
3	4
5	6

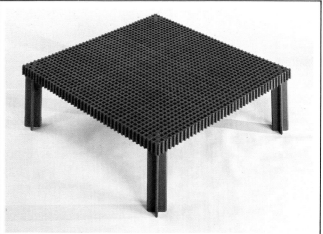

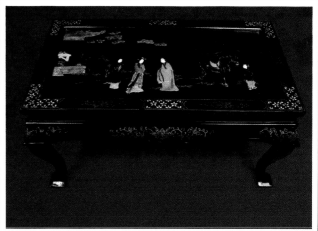

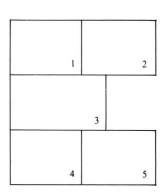

1 *Summit Tables by Castelli*
2 *Kioto Coffee Table by Sunar*
3 *Florence Knoll Conference Table by Knoll International*
4 *Letton Occasional Tables by Intrex*
5 *Chinese Lacquered Coffee Table by Oriental Imports*

1		2
	3	
4		5

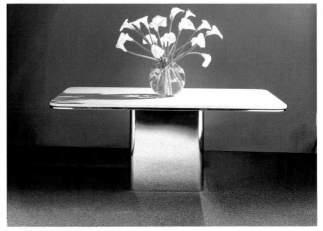

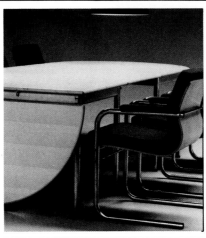

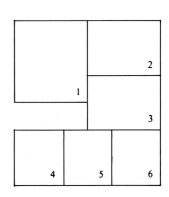

1 *Domino Table Components by Rudd International (table configuration)*
2 *Domino Table Components by Rudd International (desk configuration)*
3 *Anello Conference Table by Brueton*
4 *4022-72 Table by Dunbar*
5 *Series 2R Table Desk by Domore*
6 *4720-4721 Drum Tables by Dunbar*

1 *Sheraton Conference Table by Smith & Watson*
2 *Georgian Rent Table by Smith & Watson*
3 *Radial Table by Brueton*
4 *18th Century Satinwood Conference Table by Baker, Knapp, & Tubbs*
5 *Albert Herbert Table by Baker, Knapp & Tubbs*
6 *Sheraton Writing Table by Wodd & Hogan*

1	2
3	4
5	6

CABINETRY AND WOODWORKING

Since the handcrafting of wood predates modern technology, it suggests a sense of the past—of tradition—of having been established "forever." Used in an executive area, it implies a slower, more gracious pace—a recognition that decision making can be a lengthy process.

Wherever architectural woodworking and built-ins are used in a corporation, they are a sign of prestige—noting that the office and its occupant are here to stay. Whether it is true or not, visitors get the impression that the design is the result of the occupant's preferences. While the rank and file in a corporation may be discouraged from bringing in personal belongings, the executive is encouraged—the cabinetry providing a formal setting for prized collections and rare one-of-a-kinds. People with power are expected to stake out their territorial claims with personal possessions.

Despite the widespread use of plastic laminates with wood grain finishes, which have their legitimate applications, cabinetry and woodworking retain a special quality that comes from handicraft. It is most visible in the details: the reveals between wall panels, the joinery of moldings, frames, drawers and chair rails, the dark lucidity of aging wood. These are forms that plastic laminate was never intended to create. For the centuries-old romance of mankind and woodworking continues.

Fine details reminiscent of the American Arts and Crafts movement and the so-called Mission Style make a fireplace of African mahogany and red granite a work of sculpture in the study of the American Academy of Arts and Sciences, Cambridge (MA). The designers were Kallman, McKinnell & Wood with Louis Beal and Joseph Rosen of ISD. (Photograph by Jaime Ardiles-Arce)

OPPOSITE

Running the full 52 feet of a main reception room is a figured mahogany storage wall that defines the fine furnishings visitors see at the offices of GFI/Knoll, New York, designed by Skidmore, Owings & Merrill, San Francisco. (Photograph by Jaime Ardiles-Arce)

The reception area for the executives offices of Texas Commerce Bancshares (OPPOSITE ABOVE) and the office of its chairman (ABOVE) in Houston are formally stated by the use of architectural paneling in warm American cherry. The use of architectural woodwork by 3D/International prevails in the Bank's modern offices as well. (Photograph by Hedrich-Blessing)

LEFT
Tawny African rosewood is used to make a 24-inch deep storage wall that is accented by brass hardware for files, closets and the doors to private perimeter offices at Brobeck, Phleger and Harrison, attorneys, San Francisco, designed by Gensler and Associates. (Photograph by Jaime Ardiles-Arce)

SYSTEMS

It is difficult to imagine a time when open plan furniture systems did not exist. They, like jet travel, have become an accepted part of corporate life. Originally, systems were preferred over fixed and movable walls because they were tax write-offs, but this is no longer true since the building itself can be written off in fifteen years. Today, systems save money because they allow space to be reconfigured economically, allow more people per square foot, and save the expense of enclosed offices for middle management. They cost more to buy than standard office furniture, but this must be weighed against lower *operating* costs.

Systems do require new office etiquette and new solutions to the problems of visual and acoustical privacy. And some questions are yet to be answered. We know that systems increase employee communication, but how much is work-related communication? And does this increase in communication affect the way employees work together? (In other words, is the payoff increased efficiency?) Another question concerns young managers—what kind of future rewards can they expect now that they no longer receive an "office of one's own with a door"?

With the great variety of systems on the market today, choosing one can prove difficult unless a company has defined its needs.

Systems may or may not have the following features.

- **Functional or decorative options** can be used to create highly individualized or upgraded work stations (particularly important for higher level employees).

- **Acoustical surfaces and sound masking systems** are used to block sound or make it unintelligible.

- **Reconfiguring ease** is important if work stations are moved frequently. (A 1977 General Services Administration study found that the time required to take apart and reassemble work stations varied widely.)

- **The look of quality furniture** is available from some manufacturers who design their systems to resemble traditional furniture styles.

- **Built-in lighting,** task and/or ambient, gains flexibility from standard lighting by directing light where it is actually needed—not just where the first office design indicated. Less light wasted means energy savings as well.

- **Adjustable work surface and seating heights,** especially important when using electronic equipment such as word processors and CRTs, can result in more comfort for workers and better productivity.

- **Glare-free surfaces** prevent light from reflecting directly into the eyes.

A configuration of open plan systems furniture at Weyerhaeuser Technology Center, Tacoma (WA), designed by Skidmore, Owings & Merrill, San Francisco, has a vivacious spirit owing to the careful use of different design techniques. Among these are the 45-degree angling of furniture to building, a soft, pleasing color scheme, 24-foot ceilings, indoor plants and a view of the forest outside the Center. (Photograph by Jaime Ardiles-Arce)

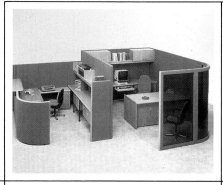

1 *Beta System by Alma*
2 *RJ System by Rose*
3 *Office System by Panel Concepts*
4 *S/4 Series™ by Dunbar*
5 *Open Plan System by GF Furniture Systems*
6 *Stephens System by Knoll International*
7 *Zapf System by Knoll International*
8 *Ultronic 9000 System by Steelcase*
9 *Office System by Modern Mode*
10 *Action Office by Herman Miller*
11 *Options System by Helikon*

	1	2
3	4	5
6	7	8
9	10	11

1	2	3
4	5	6
7	8	9
10	11	

FLOORING

Glowing colors make the Herbert Bayer carpet created for Anaconda headquarters, Denver, the center of attention in the executive reception area designed by Neville Lewis Associates and Kaneko-Laff Associates. (Photograph by Jaime Ardiles-Arce)

Flooring can pull areas together or set them apart. The use of one continuous material suggests that areas are equal in importance and equally accessible, whereas the use of accent flooring suggests that special areas exist. Sometimes the accent area is of a different material, othertimes it may only be a change of color or pattern.

The material itself is a clue to the activity of the space, since it is the one material that is always in contact with the users. Thus, rubber flooring and vinyl tile suggest a high traffic area—one that is expected to take punishment and get dirty. Carpet denotes a more relaxed, contemplative and higher status area because it is softer underfoot and therefore quieter.

Flooring must be practical above all other concerns. Carpet tiles are increasingly being used in open plan areas where regular access to underfloor wiring is necessary, or where furniture is always being moved. And low-maintenance flooring is usually chosen for lobby and reception areas where combinations of stone, stone pavers, brick, ceramic and quarry tiles, wood and carpeting can create dramatic statements.

The possibilities for custom detailing are infinite. Corporations can incorporate product colors and company logos in their flooring designs. The floors are noticed by anyone who watches where he is going.

Rugged industrial grade rubber flooring contributes a rich texture and reflectivity to the laboratory space at Noxell Corp., Cockeysville (MD), designed by the Kling Partnership. (Photograph by Ron Solomon/Eileen Brown © 1983)

RIGHT

Against a hardwood floor in a herring-bone pattern, an Oriental runner looks especially effective at the offices of Charfoos & Charfoos, attorneys, Detroit, by Jeanne Hartnett & Associates. (Photograph by Yuichi Idaka)

BELOW

Juan José Diaz-Infante and The Display Center applied marble to the atrium floor at Bufete Industrial, Mexico City, for visual interest. (Photograph by Timothy Hursley © The Arkansas Office)

ABOVE LEFT
As part of the Mexican colonial theme at Oak Industries, Rancho Bernardo (CA), Dale Naegel Architecture and Planning and Brenda Mason Design Associates tiled the main lobby. (Photograph by Charles Schneider)

ABOVE RIGHT
Checkerboard vinyl tile and carpet recall the formal nature of the Bar Counsel, Boston, designed by Charles G. Hilgenhurst Associates. (Photograph by Herb Engelsberg © 1980)

ABOVE
A grid patterned carpet helps enliven the dining at Continental Telecom, Atlanta, designed by Cooper, Carry & Associates and Ferry-Hayes Designers. (Photograph by Jonathan Hillycr)

WALL TREATMENTS

Not too many years ago, the walls of corporations were plastered and painted white and that was that. It was a neutral background for everything else. Today, an enormous variety of treatments draws attention to the walls themselves.

All manner of fabric, leather and carpet cover walls now, in addition to the paper and vinyl wallcoverings of the past. In high traffic areas, ceramic and clay tiles, metal panels, plastic laminate, and rubber are used, as well as rougher cinderblock and brick. There is also a renewed interest in glass block. While it was used for window glazing in the 1930s, today it is increasingly used for the wall itself, as is clear glass.

White is highly reflective and hard on the eyes. Soft color has now replaced pure white walls in many corporations, with a slightly stronger color used on key walls to rest the eyes. Bright color and bold treatments such as photomurals and wall graphics are used in non-work areas to lift the spirits.

Luminosity and movement are emphasized in the wall treatments for an executive support space at Evans Partnership/Evans Shure Construction, Parsippany (NJ), designed by Gwathmey Siegel & Associates using glass block, glass, photomural and painted drywall. (Photograph by Otto Baitz)

OPPOSITE
A conference area looks very much like a machined object at Wang Labs' New York offices designed by SCR Design Organization, due to the application of rubber wall covering. (Photograph by Mark Ross)

U.S. Trust's grand staircase in its renovated New York townhouse office is enriched by a special flock wallcovering chosen by Haines, Lundberg, Waehler. (Photograph by George Cserna)

OPPOSITE ABOVE
Bricks assume distinctive forms at Standard Brands Research Center, Wilton (CT), designed by Warren Platner Associates. (Photograph by © Ezra Stoller/ Esto)

OPPOSITE BELOW
To cover the rounded walls enclosing private offices at BEA Associates, New York, designer Tod Williams & Associates chose a textured silk fabric. (Photograph by Mark Ross)

UPHOLSTERY

Upholstery fabrics, like many wall coverings, are extensions of clothing that "dress" the room. Like clothing, it is a clue to character. And like flooring, it is a material that users contact.

With the great choice of colors, textures and patterns available in upholstery materials today, one can make the furniture the center of attention or let it fade quietly into the background. And while leather is long-lasting and a traditional favorite, fabrics are generally considered to be more comfortable. Natural fabrics such as wool, mohair, cotton, linen, and silk have been prestigious for centuries, but do require greater care than the synthetic fibers such as acetate, acrylic, modacrylic, nylon, olefin, polyester and rayon.

Protective finishes for fabrics are available which encourage soil resistance and release. These can be applied to the fabric before or after upholstery, but are most effective when applied at the mill. Either way, they widen the choice of fabrics. Upholstery is also rated for fire and flame resistance.

The serpentine form of a sectional seating unit is covered in leather for comfort, beauty and durability in this reception area designed by 3D/International as part of its own headquarters in Houston. (Photograph by Jaime Ardiles-Arce)

LEFT
Fabrics specifically designed for commercial or "contract" use come in a wide array of colors, weaves, fibers and weights. (Photograph courtesy of Boris Kroll)

OPPOSITE
Among the more striking objects in the antique collection on the executive floor of Continental Telecom, Atlanta, are a pair of Chippendale chairs covered in a lustrous damask. (Photograph by Mark Ross)

LIGHTING, WINDOWS AND CEILINGS

OPPOSITE

Lighting in a variety of forms subtly alters the mood during the day at the American Academy of Arts and Sciences, Cambridge (MA), designed by Kallman, McKinnell & Wood with Louis Beal and Joseph Rosen of ISD. Draped fabric prevents glare from the skylight. (Photograph by Jaime Ardiles-Arce)

Tod Williams & Associates designed a distinctive fixture incorporating fluorescent lamps flashing upwards through slotted metal tubes towards a plywood cove at BEA Associates offices in New York. This is supplemented by outdoor light visible at the end of the corridor. (Photograph by Mark Ross)

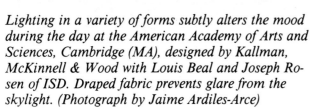

Lighting serves two purposes—to illuminate a task and to establish a mood. In most corporations, the higher the level of illumination, the less cerebral the task and therefore the lower the status. Work which involves decision making and long-term strat-egy receives lower levels of lighting because much of the effort is neither directly received nor transmitted on paper.

Natural lighting is preferred for its soft and changing qualities and because, psychologically, people like to have an external point

High pressure sodium task/ambient pendant fixtures throw light that is glare free and economical for the offices of Georgia Power Co., Atlanta, designed by Heery & Heery. The yellow cast of the light requires employees to adjust their color values to account for the inevitable distortion. (Photograph by Paul G. Beswick)

OPPOSITE

From the executive reception area of J. Walter Thompson, New York, designed by Griswold, Heckel & Kelly, can be seen many different kinds of light flooding the atrium—daylight from a skylight, high intensity diffusion (HID) lamps playing on indoor plants, and recessed ceiling incandescent down lights. (Photograph by Robert Perron)

of reference—an outdoor view—to tell the weather and time of day. Unchanging artificial lighting is, unfortunately, the norm for the majority of workers. Since many people find fluorescent lighting unpleasant, despite its economy, incandescent lamps should be considered for task lighting. The use of brass, glass, and Oriental table and floor lamps in executive offices gives employees lighting they can individually adjust, besides suggesting a warm, residential look.

Lighting shapes the look and feel of spaces as it selectively highlights certain areas and plays down others. Its effect is a combination of the natural light from windows and skylights, artificial lighting, and the ceiling treatments. When ceilings are white or of a reflective surface, they bounce light back down into the space; when they are dark-colored and matte-finished, they absorb light.

Besides plaster and acoustical tile, ceilings may be covered in glass, mirror, metal tiles, wood, pressed tin, and reflective metal strips or tile. Exposing the ducts and pipes, steel beams or pre-cast concrete tees and coffers can open up a ceiling and add a sense of sculpture.

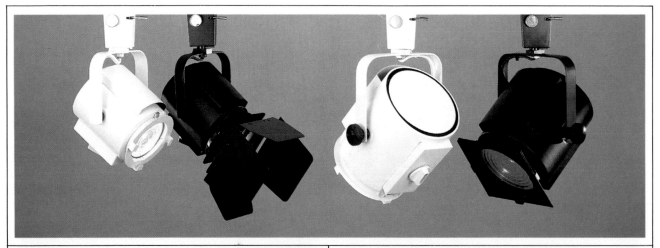

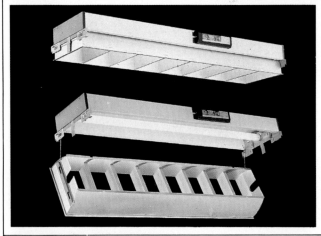

1 *Track Lighting by Lightolier*
2 *Visionair Parabolic Lamp by Edison Price*
  (Photograph by Peter L. Goodman)
3 *Barbini Table Lamp by Lighting Associates*
4 *"Eye Shade" Lamps by Koch & Lowy*

1 *Frisbee Pendant Lamp by Atelier International*
2 *NT821 Table Lamp by Nessen Lamps*
3 *"Wall" Sconce by Atelier International*
4 *Beehive Collection by Boyd Lighting*
5 *Tizio Table Lamp by Artemide*
6 *Pausania Table Lamp by Artemide*
7 *TF-360 Sconce by Rambusch*
8 *Aegean I Floor Lamp by Boyd Lighting*

1	4	7
2	5	
3	6	8

TECHNOLOGY

The trading room at Deutsche Bank, New York, designed by Interior Concepts, is part of a sleek modern design that encloses all the Bank's office equipment in neat technological packages. The custom work table is designed for the traders' convenience with easily reached controls and glare-free CRT screens. (Photograph by Jaime Ardiles-Arce)

Since modern technology is strictly utilitarian, the question for corporations is how to relate the needs of the machine to those of the organization. The physical relationship between workers and their machines will continue to be a problem as people spend increasing amounts of time dealing with each other through machines. Improving the comfort of sitting at word processors, CRTs, computers and printout units for long hours would be best dealt with as a combined effort between corporations and manufacturers.

If these machines become a way of life for all of us, from the top executive on down, the machines as well as the furniture must become more adjustable, and thus more "friendly." Even now, there is a growing need for executive furniture that will accommodate the new technology. In this transition period, as information technology makes its way into the office, some corporations will choose to conceal their machines while others will proudly display them.

INA/CIGNA's investment management offices in Philadelphia, designed by Venturi, Rauch and Scott Brown, were created to function as modern facilities using traditional materials, as this trading room intended for client viewing demonstrates. (Photograph by Tom Bernard)

The computer room at Bufete Industrial, Mexico City, designed by Juan José Infante-Diaz, is typical of computer rooms everywhere: raised floor for cable feeding, no partitions except those enclosing the room, high lighting level for detailed reading and extensive air conditioning. (Photograph by Timothy Hursley, © The Arkansas Office)

A splash of color, an interesting geometry of floor planning, and careful lighting to avoid glare results in this CRT environment at Prudential Eastern Operations, Parsippany (NJ) by Grad Partnership and Daroff Design. (Photograph by Tom Crane)

To give privacy and comfort to telephone users on the executive floor of International Paper, New York, The Space Design Group created these acoustically protected kiosks. (Photograph by Mark Ross)

Specially designed electronic work stations were needed for USA Today, Gannett Co.'s national newspaper in Rosslyn (VA), designed by Environmental Planning and Research, since the staff works entirely by computer. (Photograph by © Peter Aaron/Esto)

V Creating the Corporate Image

*"Make no little plans; they have no magic
to stir men's blood."*
—DANIEL HUDSON BURNHAM

The image of a good corporate office is as calculated as a stage set. Being a costly investment, it must balance the corporation's objective (or "functional") need to get its tasks accomplished against its subjective (or "aesthetic") desire to present an image that enhances the meaning of the tasks and those who perform them. Being a cooperative effort between the corporation and professional designers, it obliges corporate executives to express their long term strategic goals in terms that designers can comprehend and translate into office space. An oft-repeated truism from schools of design may be repeated here: good design requires good clients as well as good designers.

A design problem must be solved both technically and aesthetically. It is *almost* enough to create so many offices, conference rooms and reception areas; to design to the latest standards of architecture, engineering, interior design and ergonomics (the science of human factors); to establish a budget and a timetable for project completion.

What is missing? Ergonomic standards, for one, are far from specific given the wide range of personal preferences for softer or harder seats, quieter or noisier rooms, darker or brighter colors and so forth, from which each organization must decide. Purely functional needs can often be satisfied in numerous equally valid ways; whether a building is clad in metal, stone, glass or concrete is largely a question of cost. Budgets generally permit monies to be shifted from one area to another to concentrate modest expenditures where the company wants them to show: facade, lobby, executive offices, and cafeteria, for example.

Some design variables are purely discretionary since they do not affect function at all; corporate art and indoor plants fall in this category. And even a dysfunctional design feature can be included with the aid of environmental controls, such as a skylight atrium in a hot climate, if the corporation and its designers want it for symbolic reasons.

With so many variables in the composition of a design, a corporation can achieve a unique corporate image without financial penalties. The aesthetic outcome will naturally vary with the skill and creativity of the designers and the level of taste of the company's executives. Among the basic design tools business can use to shape the corporate office and its image are orientation, scale, proportion, form, materials, light and color.

ORIENTATION COMMANDS RESPECT

How we approach, move through and depart from a building complex or a single room is arranged by designers to set us at a particular psychological distance to it. There are numerous techniques to render an object more awe-inspiring and less familiar. We can face an object frontally, which allows us to see the full extent of its principal features; we can catch our first glimpse of the object from a great distance, which enables us to indulge our fantasies about it; we can view it from vast heights or depths, maintaining a psychological gap. Every major monumental complex, such as the Acropolis of Classical Greece, Chichen Itzá of the Toltecs, Karnak of ancient Egypt or the Forbidden City of Imperial China, plays on some of these motifs. They can also be seen

Peking is a city formed by the merging of two cultures, the Yuan (Tatar) to the north and the Chinese to the south. A wall was erected around it in 1564, and then the traditional Processional Way was constructed as the central north-south axis of the city. The northern terminus of the road is the site of the imperial palaces of the Ming, the "Forbidden City." The majesty of this famous grouping owes a good deal to the careful symmetrical aligning of the many buildings, gateways, plazas and terraces that lead visitors to the center of China's Celestial Empire. The cumulative effect inspires awe and respect, which the Forbidden City clearly does. (Photograph by Christine Simpson)

A rigid adherence to axial orientation and careful orchestration of heights and distances by the many builders of the temple of Amon-Ra at Karnak (Dynasties XVIII-XXV, 1580-633 B.C.) make the progression through its districts an almost hypnotic and supernatural event. (Photograph by Martin R. Munitz)

The Toltec buildings of Chichen Itzá rise boldly at the centers of vast esplanades. Thus, the city's masterpiece, the Castillo or Temple of Kulkulkán, looks so imposing, though it is not the largest of its type of temple architecture by any means. (Photograph courtesy of the Mexican National Tourist Council)

In the Acropolis at Athens, whose plan was established by the late 5th century, B.C., individual buildings oriented to a processional path formed a powerful ensemble that stood symbolically at the highest point of the city. (Photograph courtesy of the Greek National Tourist Office)

228

Chartres Cathedral's (LEFT) French Gothic masonry structure uses bearing walls to take the weight of the building directly to the earth. By contrast, the Sears Tower (RIGHT) in Chicago by Skidmore, Owings & Merrill, Chicago, conceals its steel structure in a thin wall of glass and metal that bears no weight. (Photograph of Chartres Cathedral courtesy of the French Government Tourist Office; photograph of Sears Tower courtesy of Sears Roebuck and Co.)

in the interiors of the leaders of church, state and commerce, such as the interior of the church of Hagia Sophia in ancient Byzantium, the grand stairway of Wurzburg Residenz in Baroque Germany or the public lobby of the Woolworth Building, in New York.

SCALE AND POWER

Our ability to estimate the size of an object comes from relating it to the dimensions of the human body, using such indicators as doors, windows and furniture. Paradoxically, the lack of ornamentation in modern design can detract from its occasionally immense size because it often offers no clue to how tall a viewer would stand beside it. The sharply differentiated elements of the west front of Chartres Cathedral, for example, seem to soar higher than the smooth facets of the Sears Tower, the world's tallest building. The rise of the Gothic structure to its two asymmetrical spires is staged as parallel but separate ascents in which buttresses, piers and pilasters lift the masonry to heights of weightless delicacy that appear to rush to the heavens at the final moment. By contrast, the flush metal and glass skin of the Sears Tower shows no sign of scale, stress or change as the structure rises, dropping off large rectilinear volumes of space before halting abruptly at its flat roofline.

PROPORTIONS AS EXTENSIONS OF MAN'S BODY

Harmonious proportions in a building or room are usually unnoticed by the casual observer; what draws his attention are propor-

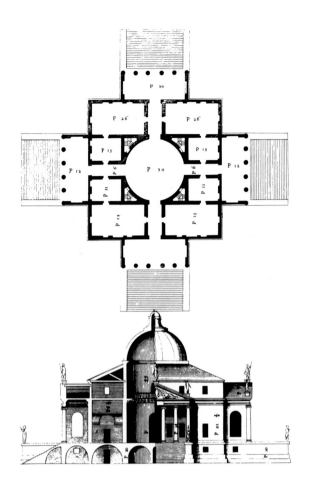

Harmonious proportions in a building or room are usually unnoticed by the casual observer; what draws his attention are proportions that appear to ignore or deliberately violate what seems most natural. We perceive proportions as the arithmetic or geometric rules that relate the dimensions of each element of a form to those of another and to the whole. In this house ("La Rotonda") for a gentleman of Vicenza by Andrea Palladio, an architect of the Renaissance and one of the most influential of all time, can be seen its designer's belief in a universally applicable body of rules governing architectural composition; its proportions are superbly balanced. (Drawing from The Four Books of Architecture *by Andrea Palladio, 1965 edition, New York: Dover Publications, Inc.)*

tions that appear to ignore or deliberately violate what seems most natural. We perceive proportions in every object, manmade or natural, as the arithmetic or geometric rules that relate the dimensions of each element of a form to those of another and to the whole. Whether a room is lofty or low, spacious or tight, rational or idiosyncratic, static or dynamic, graceful or clumsy depends on the interrelated measurements that describe it.

Ludwig Mies van der Rohe, one of Germany's distinguished masters of Modern architecture, remarked that it was not necessary to re-invent architectural theory every Monday morning. This has been true of the teaching of proportions since the first century B.C., when Vitruvius, the Roman architectural theorist, formulated his principles of the Classical orders: Doric, Ionic and Corinthian. His writings have endured for centuries, based as they are on timeless concepts such as the intensification of structural stress as the weight of a building descends to earth, and the vertical expression of form under that stress.

When proponents of Modern architec-

ture finally broke the Vitruvian rules, they often created their own, most notably the Modulor, a system of proportions based on human anatomy propounded by the legendary French architect, Le Corbusier. Hard and fast formulas no longer prevail in the design world. Commerce, however, frequently insists on maintaining the five-foot square planning module, the eight-foot ceiling, the fifteen-foot deep private office and other common practices for all but the most exceptional situations.

FORM'S HIDDEN MESSAGE

Business people who know next to nothing about aesthetic form have responded warmly to the traditional forms of 18th and 19th century English and French design. Though they may not care about cornices, chair rails or cabriole legs, they are intensely aware of these shapes as symbols of tradition, endurance and power. Executives frequently reserve the artifacts of vanished aristocracy for themselves even as the rest of their organizations occupy more modern looking facilities.

These executives are not behaving irrationally or egotistically, as is often supposed by designers. Their use of period styles is an attempt to reduce the tension between rapidly changing ideas in business management and technology, as advanced by their middle management and professionals, and ultimate long term judgments, which they alone must render. In a world that increasingly discourages long term thinking, executives play the uneasy role of judges even as their boards and shareholders put them on quarterly trial. Cloaking themselves in a traditional environment strengthens their role as final arbiters, who must consider all short term actions in the context of their companies' historic goals.

Form is thus a carrier of cultural messages from the past and present as well as the pragmatic answers to the needs of function. In its more contemporary guises, it still represents a forcible molding of function by cultural preference. Modern architecture and interior design can look like high technology apparatus, abstract geometric sculpture or pastiches of archeological fragments (ironically called "Post-Modern" design), but their surfaces mask identical technological systems hidden within. Technology's aesthetic is a neutral spirit that awaits culture to impart social character and a definitive shape.

Some 60 years were to pass before the heirs to the Modernist tradition in design could recognize the neutrality of technology. The early Modern designers held that decoration and other elaboration of form were guilty of more than simple interference with the machine; they corrupted the soul. Wrote an angry young Viennese architect, Adolf Loos, in *Ornament and Crime* in 1908, "The nomadic herdsmen had to distinguish themselves by various colors; modern man uses his clothes as a mask. So immensely strong is his individuality that it can no longer be expressed in articles of clothing. Freedom from ornament is a sign of spiritual strength."[1]

How quickly Western civilization tired of this puritanical severity was pointed out by the urban planning scholar, Christopher Tunnard, in *The Modern American City* in 1968.

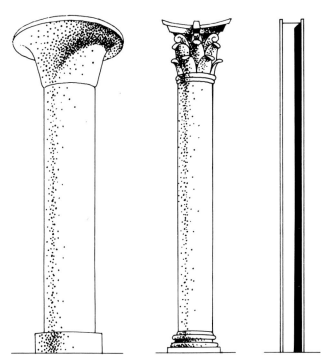

Forms such as the three columns pictured here, a campaniform capital and massive shaft from dynastic Egypt, a graceful tripartite Renaissance column, and an I-beam of modern design, signify both our changing cultural values and our growing faith in our technological prowess. This dual role is played out in almost every human artifact.

While many building materials may be technically interchangeable, their visual imagery is often quite different. Masonry, for example, is massive in weight, requires field labor to erect, and cannot span long distances. However, it performs well in compression, imparts color and texture, and can even be taught to fly—as semi-circular, elliptical or pointed arches.

In his account of the Beaux Arts Roman-style architecture that swept across the United States in the years 1893-1910, he observed, "As one travels the country today, the extraordinary quality of the City Beautiful architecture, not only in these government buildings, but in civic structures like clubs and banks, stands out to be admired among the blank faces of the newer commercial buildings, bereft as the latter are of ornament or any human touch in the form of sculpture or decoration."[2]

It is only fair to add that the best examples of Modern design were never enslaved to technological rationales. The master works themselves speak of a polyglot of creative visions that surely do not confirm the supremacy of any absolute or perfect form. What distinguishes design today from the dawn of the Modern movement is that culture's role in shaping form out of function can be freely acknowledged as the artistic act that it is. Touché, Mr. Loos.

MATERIALS HAVE STATUS

Twentieth century advertising reveals a deep ambivalence in industrial society toward handicraft and manufacture. Against predictable words such as "new," "advanced," "improved" and "state-of-the-art" range concepts such as "hand-crafted," "homemade," "natural" and "traditional." We want technical products to perform as proficiently as science and engineering will allow. On the other hand, we value a high labor content in non-technical goods and services.

That many artifacts refuse to fall neatly into either camp can often be detected in the use of materials. The confusion shows up in amusing examples like the aircraft of World War II sporting painted "nose art," typically pin-up girls or ferocious eyes and mouths, truck cabs with lavishly appointed interiors, and stereophonic equipment and other electrical devices in simulated wood-grain cabinets. Using a material "honestly" becomes a way of reinforcing the shape and function of the object it will become; using it "dishonestly" attempts to alter the impact of the final result by making it seem like something it is not.

The choice of materials measures quality in terms most of us can innately sense.

Materials such as wood, stone and fiber are "natural" in origin whereas metal, glass and plastic are "synthetic," and the difference is one of varying degrees of personal involvement by the makers of the final product. As natural materials are formed by nature and then modified by handicraft, they represent the efforts of a small group of craftsmen taking full responsibility for their work, and tend to be relatively expensive. Synthetic materials, by contrast, are fabricated by highly mechanized processes, so that while the original molds, dies and templates may be handcrafted, the final product is mass-produced and is priced accordingly. As a result, wood paneling and furniture, carpeted floors with wood or stone border trim, fabric wallcoverings and upholstery and framed original art enjoy high status in industrial society and are hallmarks of executive quarters. When they are distributed to lower echelons of the corporation, they often express an elevation of status, an egalitarian style of management or a sign of success.

Materials have other intrinsic qualities that help define the corporate image. Their colors can be warmer or cooler, solid or patterned, lighter or darker; their textures can range from manmade surface markings to machined polishes; their hardness can range from very soft to rock hard, all to support a desired degree of formality and comfort. Choosing the "right" materials is an aesthetic and political exercise as well as a functional one.

LIGHT AND COLOR CONTROL OUR PERCEPTION

The tangible world of objects and colors enters our consciousness on a stream of light. No architectural or interior design is complete until we know how light will model its features. (The French architect Le Corbusier described his profession as "the masterly, correct and magnificent play of masses brought together in lights . . . ."[3]) To control light is to control man's perception of his visible environment.

While natural light must be regarded as idiosyncratic and only partly tamable, most aspects of light are readily controlled: brightness, focus, direction and distribution. Increasing brightness makes small details easier to read; focusing on a specific area makes it stand out from its surroundings; bouncing light indirectly on a surface removes glare and harsh shadows; distributing light only on work surfaces reduces the total energy used without necessarily impairing vision. Playing these variables off one another, a company and its designer can conserve energy, establish a high degree of visual comfort and create far more interesting lighting compositions than the uniform ceiling patterns of the past. Where the traditional emphasis was on the quantity of light, the Oil Embargo of 1973 has re-oriented technological society to the quality of light. Light is both a functional and an aesthetic solution to seeing what we want to see.

Color is likewise a powerful force in shaping the office. Color programs for consumer products show how a simple change of color can dramatically alter buyers' attitudes toward otherwise similar articles like home appliances, clothing and furniture. The choice of color scheme can also be used to bolster the corporate image. The parts of a building or room can be articulated with complementary colors or suppressed with a monochromatic palette to emphasize complexity of surface or solidity of mass; darker or cooler colors can foster formality and calm; patterns of color on an object can break up its sense of weight. Color superimposes its values on everything. In this sense, there is no such thing as a "neutral" color.

TRUTH IN CORPORATE IMAGERY

Creating an effective corporate office facility—a highly functional space shaped in the image of the corporation—calls for an understanding not unlike that of a marriage or business partnership. From the corporation: a genuine commitment of adequate human and financial resources to develop the corporate facility as diligently as it does a new product. From the professional designer: a willingness to comprehend and respect the nature of the corporation's business before attempting to design anything.

A major corporate facility development project proceeds in three stages, during which the number of people and the diversity of their backgrounds, the time and money involved, and the number of key decisions to be made rise to a climax only to subside again. The process is generally irreversible, in that undoing what has been done will not only waste money already spent but will delay and thereby increase the cost of expenditures still pending. Each design decision imposes its own conditions on the choices that remain until the conclusion is all but certain.

Strategic planning and programming, the first stage of the project, are largely an internal affair of business since they involve soul-searching questions about the destiny of the organization and its management team, questions the organization must ask itself with or without the aid of external counsel. Only in probing its own thoughts about products, markets, resources, rivals, hopes and realistic chances, both current and future, can top management think logically about the specific need for a facility of an actual location, composition, size and ownership. And no one will know better than the chief executive officer and the building committee he typically forms and heads, just what the corporation intends to achieve in the new facility.

At this point, the facility can be described only in the most general terms.

• **Program** is the formal setting of standards by which a facility will be designed. What functions must be performed, for example; how many employees will be needed; what degree of adaptability, privacy, safety and comfort will be provided; what equipment will be used; how long the facility will serve its purpose.

• **Budget** deals with estimated and actual construction costs and design fees, tax and financing arrangements, operating costs and contingencies for cost overruns.

• **Scheduling** measures the critical steps in the life of the project that must be conducted smoothly to meet the company's chosen occupancy date—which may depend on expiring leases elsewhere.

- **Project team** is the group assembled from within and without the company who are asked to advise and assume responsibility for the development of the facility. Team members frequently chosen from within the corporation include: chief executive officer, chief financial officer, senior vice president for corporate real estate or general services, vice president for human resources, and managers of facilities, communications, data processing and purchasing. Team members from without the corporation might comprise: architect, interior designer, structural, mechanical and electrical engineers, general contractor, construction manager, real estate consultant, relocation consultant, telecommunications consultant, computer consultant, lighting designer, acoustician, landscape architect, food service consultant and art consultant.

Planning and design form the second stage of the project, bringing considerable expertise to focus on the major technical and aesthetic problems of developing a corporate facility. Some examples follow.

- **Site selection** is the identification of a suitable property for construction, after proper study of title, zoning laws, building codes and environmental impact.

- **Space planning** fits the various functional groups of the company on given floors of the building while establishing good organizational relationships, circulation patterns, vertical or "stacking" plans and principal entry points.

- **Design development** creates the needed structural, mechanical, lighting, power, heating, ventilation and air conditioning (HVAC) and information processing systems within an architecture and interior design of a particular aesthetic form.

- **Production** is the preparation of working drawings with due concern for materials and products technology, and the specifications of the particular products, materials and construction methods to be used.

At this stage, the chain of command must be firmly established from the project manager to the chief executive officer, and from the many outside consultants whose advice will be solicited to the key consultant(s) reporting to the corporation. The fact that today's major projects may routinely summon a dozen or more experts to assist in the development process makes the assignment of project responsibility more important than before. No one may seem in charge of a multi-million-dollar project until it fails.

Construction, occupancy and post-occupancy services constitute the third stage of the project. Specifications and working drawings are submitted to manufacturers, fabricators and contractors for bids; from their replies come contract awards that bind builder and owner to more or less fixed costs and completion dates.

- **Construction** follows the architect's and interior designer's working drawings with a wary eye for field conditions and for significant change orders instituted by the corporation, its consultants or others. Payments are usually made for given percentages of job completion.

- **Occupancy** is the phased moving of the corporation's personnel and equipment into the completed or nearly completed facility. This is usually preceded by employee orientation programs to introduce the staff to its new offices.

- **Post-occupancy services** are those supplied by the corporation's facilities management or general administration staff or outside consultants to fine tune the new facility, particularly in such areas as HVAC, lighting and interior design details, and to maintain and reconfigure it in accordance with the changing needs of the corporation.

Most corporations end up with the facilities they deserve. The offices may not be perfectly suited to their needs, yet they will accurately reflect management's attitudes toward its business. A company possessing a healthy respect for its personnel, products and customers and a strong sense of self-direction will express its confidence in its facility planning and design, as surely as it would in any other major undertaking. Good facilities are the result of honesty, sincerity and cooperation as well as money, manpower and time—like children brought into the world because they are wanted.

Light defines what we know of the visual world, and no architectural or interior design composition is complete until we know how light will model its features. While natural light must be regarded as idiosyncratic and only partly tamable, most aspects of light are readily controlled. How bright light is, how it is focused, in what direction it is aimed, and how widely it is distributed can all be determined by design, at least indoors. As shown in the stained glass windows at Chartres Cathedral, France, even natural light can be modified by the use of over 3,000 square yards of brilliantly colored glass. (Photograph courtesy of the French Government Tourist Office)

VI Appendix

Footnotes

On Corporations and Real Estate
[1] "Technology transfer: A policy nightmare," *Business Week*, April 4, 1983, p. 94.
[2] Paul Solman and Thomas Friedman, *Life and Death on the Corporate Battlefield* (New York: Simon and Schuster, 1982), p. 227.
[3] Keith Wheelock, *The New Dimensions of Office and Personnel Location* (Millburn, NJ: Fantus Company, 1979), p. 6.
[4] David Hamburg, *The World Transformed: Critical Issues in Contemporary Human Adaption* (New York: American Museum of Natural History, speech delivered on February 22, 1983).
[5] Ulrich Conrads, ed., *Programs and Manifestoes on 20th-Century Architecture* (Cambridge, MA: MIT Press, 1970), p. 13.
[6] Sam Singer and Henry R. Hilgard, *The Biology of People* (San Francisco: W.H. Freeman and Company, 1978), p. 43.
[7] Margaret Mead, *And Keep Your Powder Dry* (New York: William Morrow and Company, 1942), p. 21.

Corporate Architecture
[1] *The New York Times*, April 25, 1913, p. 1.
[2] Vincent Scully, *American Architecture and Urbanism* (New York: Praeger Publishers, 1969), p. 146.
[3] Katherine L. Bradbury, Anthony Downs, Kenneth A. Small, *Urban Decline and the Future of American Cities* (Washington: The Brookings Institution, 1982), pp. 68-9.

Corporate Interiors
[1] Edward T. Hall, *The Hidden Dimension* (New York: Doubleday & Company, Inc., 1966), p. 63.
[2] Jean D. Wineman, "Office Design and Evaluation," *Environment and Behavior*, Vol. 14 No. 3 (May 1982), p. 272.
[3] *Ibid.*
[4] Michael Korda, *Power! How To Get It, How To Use It* (New York: Random House, Inc., 1981), p. 76.
[5] Hall, *The Hidden Dimension*, p. 52.
[6] *Ibid.*, p. 53.
[7] Julius Panero and Martin Zelnik, *Human Dimension & Interior Space* (New York: Whitney Library of Design, 1979), p. 303-4.
[8] Franklin Becker, *The Successful Office* (Reading, MA: Addison-Wesley Publishing Company, Inc., 1982), pp. 54-64.
[9] Jack Curtis, "Improving Office Acoustics," *Corporate Design Magazine*, January/February, 1983, p. 93.
[10] *Ibid.*
[11] Wineman, "Office Design and Evaluation," p. 281.
[12] Becker, *The Successful Office*, pp. 69-70.
[13] Hall, *The Hidden Dimension*, pp. 116-129.
[14] Walter B. Kleeman, Jr., *The Challenge of Interior Design* (Boston: CBI Publishing Company, Inc., 1981), p. 89.
[15] *Ibid.*, pp. 85-6.
[16] Wineman, "Office Design and Evaluation," p. 276.
[17] *Ibid.*, pp. 277-8.
[18] Faber Birren, *Light, Color, and Environment* (New York: Van Nostrand Reinhold Company, 1982), p. 37.
[19] Wineman, "Office Design and Evaluation," p. 276.
[20] Illuminating Engineering Society of North America. *American National Standard Practice for Office Lighting* (New York: Illuminating Engineering Society of North America, 1982), pp. 1-44.
[21] Birren, *Light, Color, and Environment*, pp. 41-2.
[22] *Ibid.*, p. 42.
[23] *Ibid.*, p. 44.
[24] *Ibid.*, p. 56.
[25] *Ibid.*, p. 38.
[26] *Ibid.*, p. 57.
[27] John Pile, *Open Office Planning* (New York: Whitney Library of Design, 1978), p. 23.
[28] *Ibid.*, p. 34.

Corporate Furnishings
[1] Walter B. Kleeman, Jr., *The Challenge of Interior Design* (Boston: CBI Publishing Company, Inc., 1981), p. 113.
[2] *Ibid.*, p. 116.
[3] *Ibid.*, p. 113.
[4] Geoffrey Salmon, *The Working Office* (London: Design Council Publications, 1979), p. 24.
[5] Leslie Capek, *Transforming Your Office* (South Bend, IN: and books, 1981), p. 108.
[6] *Ibid.*, p. 109.
[7] Kleeman, *The Challenge of Interior Design*, p. 119.
[8] Margrethe H. Olson and Henry C. Lucas, Jr., "The Impact of Office Automation on the Organization: Some Implications for Research and Practice," *Communications of the Association for Computing Machinery*, Vol. 25 No. 11 (November 1982), p. 838.
[9] Kleeman, *The Challenge of Interior Design*, p. 92.
[10] *Ibid.*, p. 94.

Creating the Corporate Image
[1] Ulrich Conrads, ed., *Programs and Manifestoes on 20th-Century Architecture* (Cambridge, MA: MIT Press, 1970), p. 24.
[2] Christopher Tunnard, *The Modern American City* (New York: D. Van Nostrand Company, 1968), pp. 65-6.
[3] Le Corbusier, *Towards a New Architecture* (New York: Praeger Publishers, 1960; first edition, 1927), p. 37.

Bibliography

"America rushes to high tech for growth." *Business Week*, March 28, 1983, pp. 84-94.

Becker, Franklin. *The Successful Office*. Reading, Mass: Addison-Wesley Publishing Company, Inc., 1982.

Birren, Faber. *Light, Color, and Environment*. New York: Van Nostrand Reinhold Company, 1982.

Bradbury, Katherine L., Downs, Anthony, and Small, Kenneth A. *Urban Decline and the Future of American Cities*. Washington: The Brookings Institution, 1982.

Capek, Leslie. *Transforming Your Office*. South Bend, Indiana: and books, 1981.

Caplan, Ralph. *The Design of Herman Miller*. New York: Whitney Library of Design, 1976.

Conrads, Ulrich, ed. *Programs and Manifestoes on 20th-Century Architecture*. Cambridge, MA: MIT Press, 1970.

Cooper, Ken. *Bodybusiness*. New York: AMACOM, a division of American Management Associations, 1981.

Curtis, Jack. "Improving Office Acoustics." *Corporate Design Magazine*, January/February, 1983, pp. 93-4.

Garner, Philippe. *Twentieth-Century Furniture*. New York: Van Nostrand Reinhold Company, 1980.

Hall, Edward T. *The Hidden Dimension*. New York: Doubleday & Company, Inc., 1966.

Illuminating Engineering Society of North America. *American National Standard Practice for Office Lighting*. New York: Illuminating Engineering Society of North America, 1982.

Kleeman, Walter B., Jr. *The Challenge of Interior Design*. Boston: CBI Publishing Company, Inc., 1981.

Korda, Michael. *Power! How To Get It, How To Use It*. New York: Random House, Inc., 1981.

Kron, Joan, and Slesin, Suzanne. *High-Tech*. New York: Clarkson N. Potter, Inc., 1978.

Larrabee, Eric, and Vignelli, Massimo. *Knoll Design*. New York: Harry N. Abrams, Inc., 1981.

Larson, Jack Lenor, and Weeks, Jeanne. *Fabrics for Interiors*. New York: Van Nostrand Reinhold Company, 1975.

Le Corbusier. *Towards a New Architecture*. New York: Praeger Publishers, 1960 (first edition, 1927).

Manz, Karl. *History of Modern Furniture*. New York: Harry N. Abrams, Inc., 1979.

Mead, Margaret. *And Keep Your Powder Dry*. New York: William Morrow and Company, 1942.

Mumford, Lewis, ed. *Roots of Contemporary American Architecture*. New York: Dover Publications, 1972 (first edition, 1952).

Olson, Margrethe H., and Lucas, Henry C., Jr. "The Impact of Office Automation on the Organization: Some Implications for Research and Practice." *Communications of the Association for Computing Machinery*, Vol. 25 No. 11 (November 1982), pp. 838–47.

Page, Marian. *Furniture Designed by Architects*. New York: Whitney Library of Design, 1980.

Panero, Julius, and Martin Zelnik. *Human Dimension & Interior Space*. New York: Whitney Library of Design, 1979.

Pevsner, Nikolaus. *Pioneers of Modern Design*. Baltimore: Penguin Books Ltd., 1974 (first edition, 1936).

Pile, John. *Open Office Planning*. New York: Whitney Library of Design, 1978.

Riley, Noel, ed. *World Furniture*. London: Octopus Books Limited, 1980.

Salmon, Geoffrey. *The Working Office*. London: Design Council Publications, 1979.

Scully, Vincent. *American Architecture and Urbanism*. New York: Praeger Publishers, 1969.

Singer, Sam and Hilgard, Henry R. *The Biology of People*. San Francisco: W.H. Freeman and Company, 1978.

Solman, Paul and Friedman, Thomas. *Life and Death on the Corporate Battlefield*. New York: Simon and Schuster 1982.

Sommer, Robert. *Personal Space*. Englewood Cliffs, N.J.: Prentice-Hall, Inc., 1969.

Tunnard, Christopher. *The Modern American City*. New York: D. Van Nostrand Company, 1968.

Wheelock, Keith. *The New Dimensions of Office and Personnel Location*. Millburn (NJ): Fantus Company, 1979.

Wilk, Christopher. *Thonet: 150 Years of Furniture*. Woodbury, N.Y.: Barron's, 1980.

Wineman, Jean D. "Office Design and Evaluation." *Environment and Behavior*, Vol. 14 No. 3 (May 1982), pp. 271–98.

Interior Designers and Architects

Arquitectonica International Corp., 4215 Ponce de Leon Blvd., Coral Gables, FL 33146
(305) 442-9381

The Architectural Alliance, 400 Clifton Ave. South, Minneapolis, MN 55403
(612) 871-5703

Welton Becket Assoc., 200 West Monroe St., Chicago, IL 60606
(312) 296-2654

Eric Bernard Designs, 177 East 94th St., New York, NY 10028
(212) 876-9295

Davis Brody Associates, 100 East 42nd St., New York, NY 10017
(212) 599-7297

John Burgee Architects/Philip Johnson Consultant, 375 Park Ave., New York, NY 10022
(212) 751-7440

De Polo/Dunbar, 330 West 42nd St., New York, NY 10036
(212) 947-6645

Samuel De Santo & Associates, 140 West 57th St., New York, NY 10019
(212) 489-8760

Design Collective, Inc., 55 West Long St., Columbus, Ohio 43215
(614) 464-2882

Deupi & Associates, 1101 17th St. NW, Washington, DC 20036
(202) 872-8020

Juan José Diaz-Infante, Parral #64, Mexico 06140, Mexico D.F., 553-5324

The Display Center, Mexico City, Mexico

Ebert Hannum & Volz, One Sutter St., San Francisco, CA 94104
(415) 391-3260

Environmental Planning & Research, 649 Front St., San Francisco, CA
(415) 433-4715

Eve Frankl, 91 Bowman Drive, Greenwich, CT 06830
(203) 531-9795

Ulrich Franzen & Assoc., 228 East 45th St., New York, NY 10027
(212) 557-6700

Frank O. Gehry & Assoc., 11 Brooks Ave., Venice, CA 90291
(213) 392-9771

Gensler & Assoc., 550 Kearny St., San Francisco, CA 94108
(415) 433-3700

Sidney P. Gilbert & Assoc., 1035 Second Avenue, New York, NY 10022
(212) 888-1010

Jack Gordon Architects, 305 East 47th St., New York, NY 10017
(212) 759-8727

Griswold, Heckel & Kelly, 257 Park Ave., New York, NY 10016
(212) 254-1900

Haines Lundberg & Waehler, 2 Park Ave., New York, NY 10016
(212) 696-8500

Warren Hansen Assoc., Inc., 218 Madison Ave., New York, NY 10016
(212) 685-6948

Hardy Holzman Pfeiffer, 257 Park Ave., New York, NY 10010
(212) 677-6030

Jeanne Hartnett & Assoc., 43 East Ohio St., Chicago, IL 60611
(312) 751-0782

Heery & Heery Architects and Engineers, 880 West Peachtree St. NW, Atlanta, GA 30367
(404) 881-6645

Hellmuth, Obata and Kassabaum, 100 North Broadway, St. Louis, MO 73102
(314) 421-2000

Charles Herbert & Assoc., Fleming Building, Des Moines, IO 50309
(515) 288-9536

Charles G. Hilgenhurst Assoc., Inc., 148 State St., Boston, MA 02109
(617) 723-1770

Holabird & Root, 300 West Adams St., Chicago, IL 60606
(312) 726-5960

Interspace, Gable One Tower, 1320 South Dixie Highway, Coral Gables, FL 33146
(305) 655-6437

ISD, Inc., 305 East 46th St., New York, NY 10017
(212) 751-0800

Kallmann, McKinnell & Wood, 127 Tremont St., Boston, Mass 02108
(617) 482-5745

Kohn, Pederson, Fox, 11 West 57th St., New York, NY 10019
(212) 977-6500

LCP Assoc., 25 Tudor City Place, New York, NY 10017
(212) 986-8550

Peter A. Lendrum Assoc., 2920 East Camelback Rd., Phoenix, AZ 85016
(602) 955-2100

Stephen Levine Architects, 1133 Broadway, New York, NY 10010
(212) 243-3521

Neville Lewis Assoc., 142 East 8th St., New York, NY 10003
(212) 598-4300

The Luckman Partnership, 9220 Sunset Blvd., Los Angeles, CA 92101
(213) 274-7755

Maitland, Strauss/Behr Assoc., 80 Mason St., Greenwich, CT 06830
(203) 661-0898

Lee Manners & Assoc., 114 Liberty St., New York, NY 10006
(212) 227-9292

Brenda Mason Design Assoc., Inc., 1557 Columbia St., San Diego, CA 92101
(619) 238-1441

Metz, Train, Youngren of Arizona, Inc., 2721 North Central Ave., Phoenix, AZ 85004
(602) 277-7229

Morris/Aubry Architects, S.I. Morris Assoc., 2465 W. Alabama, Houston, TX 77027
(713) 622-1180

Murphy/Jahn Architects, 224 South Michigan Ave., Chicago, IL 60604
(312) 427-7300

Dale Naegle Architecture & Planning, Inc., 2210 Avenida de la Playa, La Jolla, CA 92307
(714) 459-2626

Christopher H.L. Owen, 330 East 59th St., New York, NY 10022
(212) 421-3441

Christopher Parker, 50 East 73rd St., New York, NY 10021
(212) 288-1739

Kenneth Parker Assoc., The Granary, 411 N. 20th St., Philadelphia, PA 19130
(215) 561-7700

I.M. Pei & Partners, 600 Madison Ave., New York, NY 10022
(212) 751-3122

Charles Pfister, Inc., One Maritime Plaza, San Francisco, CA 94111,
(415) 392-4455

Warren Platner Associates, 18 Mitchell Drive, New Haven, CT. 06511
(203) 777-6471

PLM Design, 1712 Commerce St., Dallas, TX 75201
(214) 744-0733

Richard Plumer Interior Design, 155 N.E. 40th St., Miami, FL 33137
(305) 573-5533

John Portman Assoc., 1800 Peachtree Center South, Atlanta, GA 30303
(404) 522-8811

Powell/Kleinschmidt, 115 South Lasalle St., Chicago, IL 60603
(312) 726-2208

Robinson & Assoc., Inc., Interior Architecture, 4217 Ponce de Leon Blvd., Coral Gables, FL 33146
(305) 445-0537

Kevin Roche & John Dinkeloo & Assoc., P.O. Box 6127, Hamden, CT 06517
(203) 777-7251

John F. Saladino, Inc., 305 East 63rd St., New York, NY 10021
(212) 752-2442

SCR Design Organization, 300 East 59th St., New York, NY 10022
(212) 752-8496

Gwathmey Siegel & Assoc., 475 10th Avenue, New York, NY 10018
(212) 947-1240

Skidmore, Owings & Merrill, 220 E. 42nd Street, New York, NY 10017
(212) 309-9500

Harwood K. Smith & Partners, 2900 Southland Center, Dallas, TX 75202
(214) 748-5261

The Space Design Group, 8 West 40th St., New York, NY 10018
(212) 221-7440

Edward Durell Stone & Assoc., 4 East 79th St., New York, NY 10021
(212) 734-0200

Charles Swerz & Assoc., 202 West 40th St., New York, NY 10018
(212) 921-7980

Swimmer Cole Martinez Curtis, 308 Washington Blvd., Marina del Ray, CA 90291
(213) 827-7200

Tardy & Assoc., 1725 Montgomery St. at Chestnut, San Francisco, CA 94111
(415) 362-5555

Adam Tihany International, 130 East 61st St., New York, NY 10021
(212) 355-6119

Venturi, Rauch & Scott Brown, 4236 Main St., Philadelphia, PA 19127
(215) 487-0400

Tod Williams & Assoc., 222 Central Park South, New York, NY 10019
(212) 582-2385

Photographers

Peter Aaron, Esto Photographics Inc., 222 Valley Place, Mamaroneck, NY 10543
(914) 698-4060

Russell Abraham, 17 Brosnan St., San Francisco, CA 94103,
(415) 558-9100

Jaime Ardiles-Arce, 663 Fifth Ave., New York, NY 10022
(212) 255-5052

Farshid Assassi, Assassi Productions, P.O. Box 3651, Santa Barbara, CA 93105
(805) 682-2158

Otto Baitz, P.O. Box Q, Cliffwood, NJ 07721
(201) 566-9533

Nathan Benn, 913 East Capitol St., SE, Washington, DC 20003
(202) 546-6182

Tom Bernard, Tom Bernard Photography, 4236 Main St., Philadelphia, PA 19127
(215) 487-0408

Paul G. Beswick, AIA, 4479 Westfield Drive, Mableton, GA 30059
(404) 944-8579

Roger Birn, 150 Chestnut St., Providence, RI 02903
(401) 421-4825

Steven Brooke, Steven Brooke Studios, 7910 SW 54th Court, Miami, FL 33143
(305) 667-8075

Tom Crane, Tom Crane Photographer, 859 Lancaster Ave., Bryn Mawr, PA 19010
(215) 525-2444

George Cserna, 80 Second Ave., New York, NY 10003
(212) 477-3472

Herb Engelsberg, Synch, 791 Tremont St., Box X, Boston, MA 02118
(617) 522-2154

Elliot Fine, Elliot Fine Photography, 800 Carroll St., Brooklyn, NY 11215
(212) 622-6613

Dan Forer, Forer, Inc., 1970 NE 149th St., N. Miami, FL 33181
(305) 949-3131

Rick Gardner, P.O. Box 25042, Houston, TX 77265
(713) 666-4066

Alexandre Georges, 66 Hilltop Circle, Palos Verdes, CA 90724
(415) 541-0033

Hedrich-Blessing Ltd., 11 West Illinois St., Chicago, IL 60610
(312) 321-1151

Jonathan Hillyer, 450-A Bishop St., Atlanta, GA 30318
(404) 352-0477

Greg Hursley, Greg Hursley, Inc., 718 North Ash, Little Rock, AR 72205
(501) 666-5930

Tim Hursley, The Arkansas Office, 115 East Capitol, Little Rock, AR 72201
(501) 372-0640

Yuichi Idaka, Idaka Photography, 4100 West Irving Park Rd., Chicago, IL 60641
(312) 282-7155

Howard Kaplan, HNK Architectural Photography, 2816 West Wilson Ave., Chicago, IL 60625
(312) 583-1222

Ashod Kassabian, Kassabian Photography, 127 East 59th St., New York, NY 10022
(212) 268-6480

Paul S. Kivett, Architectural Fotographics, 715 May St., Kansas City, MO 64105
(816) 421-3473

Balthazar Korab, Balthazar Korab, Ltd., P.O. Box 895, Troy, MI 48099
(313) 641-8881

Sara Lavicka, 1310 Bannock St., Denver, CO 80204
(303) 623-0709

Sheldon Lettich, 5225 Wilshire Blvd., Los Angeles, CA 90036
(213) 933-2291

Nathaniel Lieberman, Nathaniel Lieberman Studio, Ltd., 11 Lispenard St., New York, NY 10013
(212) 925-7141

Chas McGrath, 6207 Edloe, Houston, TX 77005
(713) 663-6825

Norman McGrath, 164 West 79th St., New York, NY 10024
(212) 799-6422

Joseph Molitor, P.O. Box N, Valhalla, NY 10595
(914) 946-4447

Peter J. Paige, Jr., Peter Paige Associates, Inc., 37 West Homestead Ave., Palisades Park, NJ 07650
(201) 592-7889

Keith Palmer/James Steinkamp Photographers, 35 East Wacker Dr., Chicago, IL 60601
(312) 427-7300

Al Payne, A.F. Payne Photographic, 830 North Fourth Ave., Phoenix, AZ 85003
(602) 258-3506

Richard Payne, 4500 Montrose Blvd., Houston, TX 77006
(713) 524-7525

Robert Perron, 104 East 40th St., New York, NY 10016
(212) 661-8796

Mark Ross, Mark Ross Photography, Inc., 345 East 80th St., New York, NY 10021
(212) 744-7258

Gordon Schenck, Jr., P.O. Box 35203, Charlotte, NC 28235
(704) 332-4078

Charles Schneider, 72 Half Moon Bend, Coronado, CA 92118
(619) 298-6118

Ron Solomon, Ron Solomon Associates, 424 East 25th St., Baltimore, MD 21218
(301) 366-6118

Jan Staller, Jan Staller Photo, 37 Walker St., New York, NY 10013
(212) 966-7043

Ezra Stoller, Esto Photographics Inc., 222 Valley Place, Mamaroneck, NY 10543
(914) 698-4060

Wesley L. Thompson, Wes Thompson Photography, P.O. Box 4488, San Diego, CA 92104
(619) 582-0812

Nick Wheeler, Corner of Turner and Pierce Roads, Townsend Harbor, MA 01469
(617) 597-2919

Toshi Yoshimi, Toshi Yoshimi Photography, 4030 Camero Ave., Los Angeles, CA 90027
(213) 660-9043

Associations and Societies

American Canvas Institute, 10 Beech St., Berea, OH 44017

Air Conditioning & Refrigeration Institute, 1815 N. Fort Meyer Dr., Arlington, VA 22209

American Hardware Manufacturers Association, 117 E. Palatine Rd., Palatine, IL 60067

American Institute of Architects, 1735 New York Ave., NW, Washington, DC 20006

American Iron and Steel Institute, 1000 16th St., NW, Washington, DC 20036

American Plywood Association, 7011 South 19th St., Tacoma, WA 98466

American Society of Interior Designers, 1430 Broadway, New York, NY 10018

American Society of Landscape Architects, Inc., 1900 M St., NW, Washington, DC 20036

American Society of Testing and Materials, 1916 Race St., Philadelphia, PA 19103

American Textiles Manufacturer's Institute, 1101 Connecticut Ave., NW, Washington, DC 20036

American Wood Council, 1619 Massachusetts Ave., NW, Washington, DC 20036

Architectural Woodwork Institute, 2310 S. Walter Reed Dr., Arlington, VA 22206

Associated Landscape Contractors of America, 1750 Old Meadow Rd., McLean, VA 22102

Association of Interior Decor Specialists (AIDS International), 2009 N. 14 St., #203, Arlington, VA 22201

Brick Institute of America, 1750 Old Meadow Rd., McLean, VA 22102

Building Stone Institute, 420 Lexington Ave., New York, NY 10170

Business & Institutional Furniture Manufacturer's Association (BIFMA), 2335 Burton SE, Grand Rapids, MI 49506

California Redwood Association, 1 Lombard St., San Francisco, CA 94111

Carpet Cushion Council, P.O. 465, Southfield, MI 48037

Carpet & Rug Institute, P.O. Box 2048, Dalton, GA 30720

Color Association of the U.S. Inc., 24 E. 38th St., New York, NY 10016

Color Marketing Group, 1133 Fifteenth St., NW, Washington, DC 20005

Contract Furnishings Council, 1190 Merchandise Mart, Chicago, IL 60654

Contract Manufacturers Association, 1056 Merchandise Mart, Chicago, IL 60654

Copper Development Association, 405 Lexington Ave., New York, NY 10174

Cotton Incorporated, 1370 Avenue of the Americas, New York, NY 10019

The Decorative Fabrics Association, Richard Dillon, Jr., c/o Greeff Fabrics, Inc., 155 East 56th St., New York, NY 10022

Foundation for Interior Design Education Research (FIDER), 242 W. 27th St., New York, NY 10001

Hardwood Institute, Div. National Hardwood Lumber Association, 230 Park Ave., New York, NY 10017

Illuminating Engineering Society of North America, 345 E. 47th St., New York, NY 10017

Institute of Business Designers, 1155 Merchandise Mart, Chicago, IL 60654

Institute of Real Estate Management, 430 North Michigan, Chicago, IL 60611

Interior Plantscape Association, 11800 Sunrise Valley Dr., Reston, VA 22091

International Association of Lighting Designers, 40 E. 49th St., New York, NY 10017

International Facility Management Association, 3971 S. Research Park Dr., Ann Arbor, MI 48104

International Linen Promotion Commission, 280 Madison Ave., New York, NY 10016

International Society of Interior Designers, 8170 Beverly Blvd., Suite #203, Los Angeles, CA 90048

The Italian Tile Center, 499 Park Ave., 6th Fl., New York, NY 10022

Jute Carpet Backing Council, Inc., 30 Rockefeller Plaza, New York, NY 10112

Marble Institute of America, 33505 State St., Farmington, MI 48024

Mohair Council of America, 183 Madison Ave., New York, NY 10016

National Association of Corporate Real Estate Executives, 501 Spencer Dr., West Palm Beach, FL 33409

National Association of Mirror Manufacturers, 5101 Wisconsin Ave., Suite 504, Washington, DC 20016

National Association of Realtors, 430 N. Michigan Ave., Chicago, IL 60611

National Council of Acoustical Consultants, P.O. Box 359, 66 Morris Ave., Springfield, NJ 07081

National Curtain, Drapery & Allied Products Association, Inc., P.O. Drawer F, Jamesburg, NJ 08831

National Electrical Contractor's Association, 7315 Wisconsin Ave., Washington, DC 20014

National Electrical Manufacturers Association, 2101 L St., NW, Washington, DC 20037

National Fire Protection Association, 430 Atlantic Ave., Boston, MA 02210

National Office Products Association, 301 N. Fairfax St., Alexandria, VA 22314

National Paint & Coatings Association, 1500 Rhode Island Ave., NW, Washington, DC 20005

Organization of Facility Managers & Planners International, Box 255, Blue Bell, PA 19422

Resilient Floor Covering Institute, 1030 15 St., NW, Suite 350, Washington, DC 20005

Resources Council, Inc., 979 Third Ave., Rm. 902N, New York, NY 10022

Rubber Carpet Cushion Association, 1345 Avenue of the Americas, New York, NY 10019

Society of Plastics Industry, 355 Lexington Ave., New York, NY 10017

Tile Council of America Inc., P.O. Box 326, Princeton, NJ 08540

Urban Land Institute, 1090 Vermont Ave., NW, Washington, DC 20005

Wallcovering Manufacturers Association, Box 359, 66 Morris Ave., Springfield, NJ 07081

Wool Bureau Inc., 360 Lexington Ave., New York, NY 10017

Sources